Multicultural American History Through Children's Literature

Deborah A. Ellermeyer, Ed.D.
Kay A. Chick, Ed.D.

Teacher Ideas Press
Portsmouth, NH

Teacher Ideas Press
A division of Reed Elsevier Inc.
361 Hanover Street
Portsmouth, NH 03801–3912
www.teacherideaspress.com

Offices and agents throughout the world

The author and publisher wish to thank those who have generously given permission to
reprint borrowed material:

National Standards for History published by the National Center for History in the Schools, 1996. Used by permission of the National Center for History in the Schools.

Library of Congress Cataloging-in-Publication Data

Ellermeyer, Deborah.
Multicultural American history through children's literature / Deborah A. Ellermeyer, Kay A. Chick.
    p. cm.
Includes bibliographical references.
ISBN 1-56308-955-6
1. Pluralism (Social sciences)—United States—History—Study and teaching (Elementary) 2. Ethnology—United States—History—Study and teaching (Elementary) 3. United States—Ethnic relations—Study and teaching (Elementary) 4. United States—History—Study and teaching (Elementary) 5. Children's literature, American—Study and teaching (Elementary) 6. Pluralism (Social sciences) in literature—Study and teaching (Elementary)—United States. 7. Children—Books and reading—United States. I. Chick, Kay A. II. Title.
E184.A1 E396 2003
372.89'044—dc21   2003013593

Editor: Suzanne Barchers
Production Coordination: Angela Laughlin
Typesetter: Westchester Book Group
Cover design: Joni Doherty
Manufacturing: Steve Bernier

Printed in the United States of America on acid-free paper

07 06 05 04 03 VP 1 2 3 4 5

With love and best wishes to my brothers and sisters: Ronald Sanko, Doug Sanko, Pam Salsgiver, Dan Sanko, and Sandy Beck. A special congratulations to my nephew, Deo Beck, on his high school graduation.—DAE

This book is dedicated to my family, Bill, Tyler, and Tim. Special thanks go to Tyler for his computer assistance.—KAC

Contents

Introduction

PURPOSE

Multicultural American History Through Children's Literature is an integrated teacher resource book designed to provide intermediate grade level teachers (grades 3–6) with lesson ideas for the instruction of social studies/history concepts within the context of quality multicultural children's books and picture books. Many of the books and activities, however, can be easily adapted for use in a primary classroom. Each chapter provides teachers with the titles of three picture books related to various multicultural themes in American history, covering topics in history from the 1400s when the pilgrims traveled to America to the present day. This resource book provides teachers with a brief summary of each book, a listing of limited materials needed to implement lesson activities, a listing of key concepts for each area of study, and student-centered learning activities designed to develop and enhance social studies/history concepts in accordance with the most recent history standards, which are outlined and described in the *National Standards for History* (1996) (see Appendix). Also included is a matrix that will, at a glance, identify and summarize the history standards highlighted in each of the units of study. Additional book titles and poems related to the themes are included at the end of each chapter.

RATIONALE

Why Teach Social Studies Concepts to Children?

Teaching children about social studies concepts is an essential component of every well-balanced elementary curriculum. The following four reasons have been identified by the authors of the *National Standards for History* (1996) for the inclusion of social studies and history instruction at the elementary level:

1. A knowledge of social studies/history concepts connects each child with his or her roots and develops in each child a sense of personal belonging. Children need to be aware of their own personal heritage and understand how they fit into the larger global community.

2. A knowledge of social studies/history concepts allows each child to move to an informed discriminating citizenship, which is essential to foster effective participation

in democratic processes. Learning about the characteristics of good citizenship should commence during the early elementary years and continue to be developed throughout the education of every individual.

3. A knowledge of social studies/history concepts allows a society to share core values, a common memory of where it has been, and how past decisions account for present conditions. In this sense, history is the common thread that binds the past to the present and the present to the past.

4. A knowledge of social studies/history concepts is the precondition of political intelligence. In essence, informed citizens will be better able to make intelligent decisions regarding the issues that affect them and their country.

Why Use Multicultural Picture Books to Teach Social Studies Concepts?

There are several advantages of using quality multicultural picture books to teach social studies concepts. The advantages are discussed briefly below.

1. Picture books can be used as a supplement to textbooks to arouse students' curiosity when a new unit of study is introduced. As a result of the colorful illustrations, intriguing characters, story format, manageable length, and understandable language, children are attracted to picture books. Consequently, picture books can effectively capture students' attention in a particular area of study.

2. Picture books can add depth to a specific topic by providing detailed information that is often missing from standard textbooks. Because of space constraints within a textbook, standard texts often present students with a very narrow view of historical concepts. Picture books expand students' knowledge and understanding of historical events and concepts.

3. Picture books can present students with alternative views and perspectives on specific historical events, which are often lacking in standard textbooks. In this way, picture books have the capability of more fully informing students of various viewpoints on any given historical event.

4. Picture books reveal history through the eyes of characters, either actual or fictional, who have lived through historical events, instead of through the eyes of biased and remote textbook authors. Students often find that the information presented in texts is presented in a detached and factual manner. History, when revealed through the eyes of people who lived through events and time periods, becomes more real and personal for the reader. Picture books present to children the human side of history that is lacking in standard texts.

5. Picture books lend themselves to presenting sometimes difficult or sensitive concepts to children in an age-appropriate and tasteful manner. Consequently, young students can learn about an event, such as the Holocaust, within the context of quality children's literature that has been specifically written for them.

Criteria for Choosing Multicultural Picture Books
to Use in the Teaching of Social Studies Concepts

Farris and Fuhler (1994) have identified criteria for choosing picture books to use in the teaching of social studies concepts. Additionally, Beaty (1997) has suggested guidelines for choosing appropriate multicultural picture books. Outlined below is a list of questions to be used with each picture book that is being considered for use within the elementary social studies curriculum.

1. Are the facts presented within the text authentic?

2. Are facts and opinions clearly differentiated? Arc opinions adequately supported?

3. Will the content of the picture book extend the social studies topic that is being studied?

4. Are the text and illustrations free of stereotyping?

5. Does the language or dialect show respect for the culture?

6. Is there a balance of books showing different facets of each culture?

7. Is there a variety of genres, including poetry, historical fiction, biographies, folktales and legends, and informational books?

8. Will the story, illustrations, and characters appeal to the students and is the content developmentally appropriate?

9. Are the illustrations accurate reflections of the text, the historical period, and the culture?

BENEFITS FOR TEACHERS

The benefits of using the teacher resource book *Multicultural American History Through Children's Literature* are many. Several benefits are discussed below.

1. Teaching Social Studies Concepts within the Meaningful Context of Quality Multicultural Children's Picture Books

   Picture books can bring social studies and history alive for young learners. Picture books can get children in touch with the human, feeling side of history. Whereas social studies texts have long been criticized for their rather dry and factual presentation of material, the colorful illustrations, readable text, and story format of picture books appeal to children. Learning about key historical events and people via a quality picture book makes learning a pleasurable and meaningful experience for students and teachers alike.

2. A Variety of Student-Centered Learning Activities to Develop and Reinforce Social Studies Concepts in Accordance with the National Standards for History.

   Students learn best when they are actively engaged in the learning process. The student-centered activities provided herein are designed to involve students actively in meaningful and enjoyable learning experiences while teaching essential social studies concepts. The authors identify the national history standards each unit of study addresses.

3. Integration of Other Instructional Skill Areas within Social Studies Activities

In addition to involving students in social studies and history-related activities, this resource book provides teachers with activities that effectively integrate other areas, including: math reading; writing; oral language; listening; creative dramatics; social, environmental, and community awareness; art; creative and critical thinking; problem solving; and cooperative learning. Areas of integration are clearly delineated and specified for each learning activity included in the book.

4. Ease and Versatility of Use

Multicultural American History Through Children's Literature is a teacher-friendly resource book that is easy to use. It is written in a style that teachers can easily read and understand. Each unit of study is based on quality children's picture books, most of which are accessible through school book clubs. Each unit identifies the books and other limited materials necessary to complete the activities. A brief book summary is also provided. Key concepts and areas of integration, as well as history standards, are identified for each unit of study.

The lessons can be used in a variety of ways within the social studies curriculum. The book can be used effectively by teachers who use an adopted social studies textbook and by those teachers who use a more holistic, eclectic approach to instruction. Teachers using adopted social studies texts will find the book helpful in introducing social studies themes and providing supplemental information and learning activities. Teachers with more eclectic approaches to instruction will find the book a developmentally appropriate alternative to social studies texts.

Students will enjoy the selected picture books and the creative, student-centered learning activities. The variety of books, topics, and activities will maintain the interest of students in any classroom.

5. Opportunity for Authentic, Performance-based Assessment

Through the use of this teacher resource book, teachers are afforded the opportunity to assess their students' learning via the completion of a wide variety of authentic, enjoyable, performance-based tasks. The variety of ways in which students demonstrate their understanding of concepts also recognizes and applies the theory of Howard Gardner's (1993) multiple intelligences.

TIPS ON USING THE BOOK WITH STUDENTS

1. Familiarize Self with the Picture Books in Advance of Reading to the Class

It is suggested that teachers obtain copies of the book(s) they wish to use with their students and familiarize themselves with them in advance of presenting them to the class. Since the teacher will be reading the picture books aloud to the group, only one copy of each book is required for each lesson. A pre-reading allows the teacher an opportunity to develop questions that can be used to engage listeners actively throughout the reading of the text. A pre-reading also gives the teacher an opportunity to examine closely illustrations and note points of particular interest that might be discussed with the class during the reading of the book. Finally, a pre-reading of the text helps ensure a more fluent and expressive reading in class.

2. Decide the Best Way to Use the Picture Books and Activities to Enhance Student Learning

    The picture books and accompanying lessons contained within this teacher resource book can be used in a variety of ways. They can be used by themselves or in conjunction with an adopted social studies text. The units can be used to introduce a particular social studies topic or broaden students' understanding of concepts that have already been introduced. Teachers have the option of choosing how each unit best fits into their existing social studies curriculum.

3. Read the Book Aloud to the Class

    In order to facilitate discussion and focus students' attention on key vocabulary and concepts, it is recommended that the teacher read the books aloud to the students. Begin the reading by giving students a purpose for listening. Ask students to make predictions throughout the book and check them for accuracy as the reading continues. Encourage students to reread the book on their own and suggest other books, which are listed at the end of each unit, on the same historical event or concept.

4. Prepare Lessons in Advance of Teaching

    Some of the lessons require minimal teacher preparation and materials. Necessary materials should be obtained in advance of the teaching of the lesson. Teachers can easily adapt individual lessons to meet the needs of the learners in their classrooms.

REFERENCES

Beaty, J. *Building Bridges with Multicultural Picture Books.* Upper Saddle River, NJ: Prentice-Hall, 1997.

Farris, P., and C. Fuhler. "Developing Social Studies Concepts through Picture Books." *Reading Teacher* 47, no. 5 (1994):380–87.

Gardner, H. *Frames of Mind: The Theory of Multiple Intelligences.* New York: Basic Books, 1993.

National Center for History in the Schools. *National Standards for History.* Los Angeles: University of California Press, 1996.

CHAPTER *1*

Coming to America

Building a New Land: African-Americans in Colonial America

Jim Haskins and Kathleen Benson
(New York: HarperCollins, 2001)

Book Summary: This picture book for older readers examines the lives of African-American slaves beginning in the 1400s, with an emphasis on the colonial period in America (1607–1763). From the settling of Jamestown to the slave revolts of the 1700s, the authors share the experiences, traditions, and contributions of African Americans in a changing society.

Key Concepts: Slavery, colonial America

National History Standards: 1, 5, and 6

Activity #1: Design a Postcard

Materials for Activity #1:

- Sample picture postcards from various places
- 4″ × 6″ blank white index cards (1 per student)
- Markers, crayons, colored pencils, and paint

Areas of Integration: Creative and artistic expression, oral language

After reading *Building a New Land: African-Americans in Colonial America*, ask students if they have ever gone on trips with their families. Ask if they have ever mailed a postcard to someone back home while on their trip. Following a brief discussion, show students samples of picture postcards from various places. Have students note and discuss the format of postcards.

Next, have students assume that they are slaves being brought to America. Have them design postcards to send back to relatives in their homeland that depict an aspect of their journey or new life in America. Encourage students to depict scenes detailed throughout the book.

After designing the front of the card, have students complete the back of the card by scripting messages to relatives that relate to the front illustration on their postcards. They can also create an appropriate destination name and address, as well as design a stamp for their postcards.

Activity #2: Book Making: The Contributions of African Americans

Materials for Activity #2:

- Internet access
- Library access
- Heavy 8½″ × 11″ paper
- Spiral binding
- Crayons and markers

Areas of Integration: Research skills, written expression, artistic expression

After reading and discussing the chapter "African Contributions to Colonial Society," ask students to list the contributions of African Americans in the areas of art, music, and literature and storytelling. Record students' ideas on the chalkboard or poster board. Have students expand on the contributions mentioned in the book by researching on websites or in other books. Students may also want to interview parents, grandparents, or other adults who may know of the cultural contributions of African Americans. After the list is complete, have each student select one contribution to research in more depth. Each student will then contribute a page in a class book on the contributions of African Americans. The book could be divided into three chapters: art, music, and literature and storytelling. Each page would include an artistic representation of the contribution and a short paragraph detailing the history of the item. The book could be spiral bound and placed in the library or classroom.

Activity #3: The Forced Immigration of African Americans

Materials for Activity #3:

- Large map of the world
- Pushpins
- Yarn or string

Areas of Integration: Geography skills, critical thinking

After reading and discussing *Building a New Land: African-Americans in Colonial America*, ask students to compare the native countries from which African Americans emigrated with countries from which other groups, such as Caucasian Americans and Hispanic Americans, emigrated. Students may use other reference materials or interview relatives to gather more information. Have students use pushpins and yarn to show the distance traveled from native countries to areas settled in America. As a class have students discuss the following:

1. The time period when various groups came to America

2. The reasons why various groups came to America

3. The areas where various groups settled in America

4. A comparison of experiences in the new country.

Nickommoh! A Thanksgiving Celebration

Jackie French Koller
(New York: Scholastic, 1999)

Book Summary: This is the story of the first Thanksgiving from the perspective of the Narragansett Indian tribe that lived in what is now Rhode Island. Native Narragansett language is incorporated into the telling of the story, and the author includes author's notes and a glossary at the end of the book.

Key Concepts: Thanksgiving, Narragansett Indian tribe

National History Standards: 1, 2, and 6

Activity #1: "Who has . . . ?" Vocabulary Game

Materials for Activity #1:

• "Who has . . . ?" game cards (provided)

Areas of Integration: Listening skills, auditory memory

After reading and discussing the book *Nickommoh! A Thanksgiving Celebration*, have students play the "Who has . . . ?" vocabulary game to learn the words from the Narragansett Indian tribe. Distribute the cards randomly to the students and keep card #1 for yourself. Read the first question. The student who has the answer reads it and then reads the question on his or her card. Play continues from one student to another until all the cards have been read. (Words and definitions are taken from the glossary provided in *Nickommoh! A Thanksgiving Celebration*.)

"Who has . . . ?" Vocabulary Game

Card #1: Who has a word that describes pits dug into the earth and lined with mats? Baskets of dried-foods were stored in these for winter use.	**Card #2:** *Auqunnash* Who has a word that names an arbor consisting of four poles sixteen to twenty feet high, set up in a square? Strings of wampum and other valued possessions were hung from the poles. Men then gambled for the prizes.
Card #3: *Gaming Arbor* Who has a word that means a crow, the sacred bird of the Narragansett?	**Card #4:** *Kaukant* Who has a word that is the Narragansett name for God, the Creator, who gave a spirit to all of his creations?
Card #5: *Kautantawwitt* Who has the word for soft deerskin shoes?	**Card #6:** *Mocussinass* Who has the three words for the colors red, yellow, and black? The Narragansett used these colors to paint their bodies and faces for ceremonies, war, and every day.
Card #7: *Msqui, Wesaui, Mowi-sucki* Who has the word for cornmeal, boiled in water until it is a thick pudding?	**Card #8:** *Nasaump* Who has the Narragansett word for a celebrational gathering?
Card #9: *Nickommoh* Who has the definition for winter?	**Card #10:** *Papone* Who has the word for a sweat lodge?

Card #11: *Pesuponck*

Who has the word for summer?

Card #12: *Quaqusquan*

Who has the word that names a ceremonial longhouse, sometimes 100 to 200 feet long?

Card #13: *Qunnekamuck*

Who has the word that describes the place where Native American people gather for ceremonies and dances? It is considered a sacred shape.

Card #14: *Sacred Circle*

Who has the word for spring?

Card #15: *Sequan*

Who has the word for a flat stone, rounded to a disk, which could be rolled on its edge while players hurled eight-foot poles, trying to land them as close as possible to where the disk would come to rest?

Card #16: *Spear-the-Disk*

Who has the word for the great woolly mammoth?

Card #17: *Stiff-Legged Bear*

Who has the word for October, the harvest month?

Card #18: *Taqountikeeswush*

Who has the word for crystalline stones that had been struck by lightning and were found in the ground near trees? These were thought to bring luck.

Card #19: *Thunderbolts*

Who has the word for a game in which two teams stretch a rope between them and mark the midline? Both teams try to pull the other team across the midline.

Card #20: *Tug-of-War*

Who has the word for the Pleistocene Era, when the great woolly mammoth, giant elk, caribou, musk ox, saber-toothed tiger, giant beaver, and an immense Kodiak-like species of bear inhabited New England?

Card #21: *When the Animals Were Big*

Who has the word for purple and white beads made from quahog shell, used for adornment and for money? The purple beads were rarer and worth about three times as much as the white.

Card #22: *Wompampeage or Wampum*

Activity #2: Becoming Strategic Readers

Materials for Activity #2:

• Questions to encourage strategic reading (provided)

Areas of Integration: Critical thinking, auditory memory

Before reading the book *Nickommoh! A Thanksgiving Celebration*, encourage students to become strategic readers by asking themselves the following questions:

1. What will this book be about?

2. What do the title and pictures tell me?

3. What do I already know about this topic that will help me?

4. From whose perspective is this story told?

5. Why would the author write this?

6. How might this Thanksgiving story be alike or different from other Thanksgiving stories?

After discussion, read the book. While you are reading, ask students to consider the following questions in order to improve their comprehension of the story:

1. What have I learned so far?

2. What have I found interesting so far?

3. Is this book easy to read or hard to read? Why?

4. How can I figure out difficult words or parts of the story I don't understand?

5. What strategies would help me to understand better this kind of book?

6. What is the author implying or what underlying messages is she sending?

7. How do I feel about what the author is saying?

8. How do the pictures help me to understand the story?

After you have finished reading the book, have students discuss the following questions:

1. What did I learn?

2. Were my predictions about the book correct?

3. Did I like this book? Why or why not?

4. How would I summarize what I read?

5. Are there any parts that I should read again to be sure that I understand what they meant?

6. Are there any new vocabulary words that I have learned?

7. How was this book similar to or different from other Thanksgiving stories I have read?

8. How does this Thanksgiving story compare to my own Thanksgiving experiences?

Activity #3: A Book Review of
Nickommoh! A Thanksgiving Celebration

Materials for Activity #3:
• Writing paper (1 sheet per student)

Areas of Integration: Written expression, critical thinking

After reading and discussing the book, have students write a book review of the story. Begin by sharing reviews of other books so that students learn what a book review is and how one is written. Encourage students to be very specific about what they liked and did not like about the book. After the reviews are finished, arrange students in small groups. Allow students to share and discuss their book reviews. Encourage students to justify their opinions about the book while also considering other students' perspectives.

The First Thanksgiving

Jean Craighead George
(New York: Philomel, 1993)

Book Summary: Craighead George tells the story of Squanto, a Pawtucket man, who helped save the lives of the Pilgrims by teaching them the ways of the land. This tale of the *Mayflower*'s travels to the New World, and of their first year here with the Native Americans, is the true story of the first Thanksgiving.

Key Concepts: The *Mayflower*, Squanto, Thanksgiving, Plymouth Rock

National History Standards: 1, 2, 4, 5, and 6

Activity #1: Historical Facts of the First Thanksgiving

> **Materials for Activity #1:**
>
> • Writing paper (1 sheet per student)

Areas of Integration: Critical thinking, oral language

After reading and discussing *The First Thanksgiving*, discuss with students the authenticity of Jean Craighead George's book. Ask students to list ten historical facts that they learned from the book that they did not know before. After students have made their lists, make a group list on chart paper. Then have students pretend that they are newspaper reporters who lived during this period of history. Have them write a short newspaper article describing the events of the first Thanksgiving.

Activity #2: Sharing Pumpkin Bread

> **Materials for Activity #2:**
>
> • Ingredients for pumpkin bread (see recipe)
> • Mixing bowls and spoons
> • Measuring cups and spoons
> • Loaf pans
> • Oven
> • Plastic wrap

Areas of Integration: Following directions, measuring ingredients, cooperative learning, service

After reading and discussing the book, discuss with students the importance of giving as a way to celebrate the Thanksgiving holiday. Decide on a recipe, such as the one below for cranberry pumpkin bread, that the class might make to share with people in a nursing home or homeless shelter.

Decide with students the responsibilities that each student will have (bringing in ingredients, measuring, chopping, mixing, setting the oven temperature, cleaning up, wrapping the bread, etc.). Deliver the bread to a nursing home or homeless shelter and allow time for students to talk with residents.

Cranberry Pumpkin Bread

Ingredients:

1 cup whole raw cranberries, fresh or frozen, coarsely chopped

1½ cups all-purpose white flour

¼ cup cornmeal

1½ cups granulated sugar

1 teaspoon baking soda

¼ teaspoon baking powder

¾ teaspoon salt

½ teaspoon ground cinnamon

½ teaspoon ground ginger

¼ teaspoon ground cloves

1 egg

1 cup canned pumpkin puree

4 tablespoons vegetable oil

2 teaspoons grated orange rind

Directions:

Preheat the oven to 350 degrees. Lightly coat a loaf pan with vegetable oil spray. Mix the flour, cornmeal, sugar, baking soda, baking powder, salt, cinnamon, ginger, and cloves in a large bowl. In a medium bowl whisk the egg with the pumpkin puree until smooth. Mix in the oil and orange rind. Add to the flour mixture and mix until blended. Add the cranberries and mix. Scrape the batter into the prepared pan. Bake until a toothpick comes out clean, 55 to 60 minutes. Cool in the pan for 10 minutes, turn onto a rack, and cool completely before slicing.

Activity #3: Thanksgiving Traditions

Materials for Activity #3:

- Shields, drawn on 8½″ × 11″ paper (1 per student)
- Crayons, markers, or colored pencils

Areas of Integration: Artistic expression, oral language

After reading and discussing *The First Thanksgiving*, discuss with students some of the Thanksgiving traditions they observe in their family. Give each student a shield and ask them to design the shield so that it represents their family's Thanksgiving traditions. Allow students to share their shields in a small group. Hang the shields in your classroom.

Related Books

Adler, D., and A. Wallner. *A Picture Book of Christopher Columbus*. New York: Scholastic, 1991.

Altman, S. *Extraordinary African Americans: From Colonial to Contemporary Times*. Chicago: Children's Press, 2001.

Branse, J. L. *A Day in the Life of a Colonial Sea Captain*. New York: Powerkids, 2002.

Bruchac, J. *Squanto's Journey: The Story of the First Thanksgiving*. San Diego, CA: Silver Whistle, 2000.

Dalgliesh, A. *The Thanksgiving Story*. New York: Scholastic, 1990.

Fritz, J., and J. B. Hendelsman. *Who's That Stepping on Plymouth Rock?* New York: Scholastic, 1975.

Grace, C. *1621: A New Look at Thanksgiving*. Washington, DC: National Geographic Society, 2001.

Haskin, J. *Black Stars of Colonial Times and the Revolutionary War: African Americans Who Lived Their Dreams*. Hoboken, NJ: John Wiley & Sons, 2002.

Jackson, G. *The First Thanksgiving*. New York: Scholastic, 2000.

Kalman, B. *Colonial Times from A to Z*. New York: Crabtree, 1997.

Knight, J. *The Village: Life in Colonial Times*. Mahwah, NJ: Troll, 1998.

Kroll, S., and S. D. Schindler. *Oh! What a Thanksgiving*. New York: Scholastic, 1988.

Maestro, B., *The Discovery of the Americas*. New York: Scholastic, 1991.

Maestro, G. *The New Americans: Colonial Times 1620–1689*. New York: Lothrop Lee & Shepard, 1998.

Masoff, J. *Colonial Times, 1600–1700*. Chronicle of America Series. New York: Scholastic, 2000.

McGovern, A. *If You Sailed on the Mayflower in 1620*. New York: Scholastic, 1991.

McGovern, A., and J. Luker. *The Pilgrims' First Thanksgiving*. New York: Scholastic, 1973.

Metaxas, E. *Squanto and the Miracle of Thanksgiving*. Nashville, TN: Thomas Nelson, 1999.

Moore, E. *Good Children Get Rewards: A Story of Williamsburg in Colonial Times*. New York: Cartwheel Books, 2001.

Waters, K., and R. Kendall. *Samuel Eaton's Day*. New York: Scholastic, 1993.

———. *Sarah Morton's Day*. New York: Scholastic, 1989.

Wilmore, K. *A Day in the Life of a Colonial Blacksmith*. New York: Powerkids, 2000.

———. *A Day in the Life of a Colonial Schoolteacher*. New York: Powerkids, 2000.

———. *A Day in the Life of a Colonial Silversmith*. New York: Powerkids, 2000.

Related Poetry

Allard, L. "The Three Ships." In *Poetry Place Anthology*. Ed. Rosemary Alexander. New York: Scholastic, 1990.

Clark, K. "Colonial Days." In *Poetry Place Anthology*. Ed. Rosemary Alexander. New York: Scholastic, 1990.

Dennis, E. "Like Columbus." In *Poetry Place Anthology*. Ed. Rosemary Alexander. New York: Scholastic, 1990.

Fisher, A. "First Thanksgiving." In *Poetry Place Anthology*. Ed. Rosemary Alexander. New York: Scholastic, 1990.

———. "Thanksgiving Dinner." In *Celebrating America: A Collection of Poems and Images of the American Spirit*. Ed. Laura Whipple. New York: Philomel, 1994.

Ford, M. "For Common Joys." In *Poetry Place Anthology*. Ed. Rosemary Alexander. New York: Scholastic, 1990.

Frank, B. "Were You Afraid?" In *Poetry Place Anthology*. Ed. Rosemary Alexander. New York: Scholastic, 1990.

Frost, R. "The Gift Outright." In *Hand in Hand: An American History through Poetry*. Ed. Lee Bennett Hopkins. Riverdale, NJ: Simon & Schuster, 1994.

Hemans, F. "The Landing of the Pilgrim Fathers." In *Hand in Hand: An American History through Poetry*. Ed. Lee Bennett Hopkins. Riverdale, NJ: Simon & Schuster, 1994.

Hendryx, E. "Daily Thanks." In *Poetry Place Anthology*. Ed. Rosemary Alexander. New York: Scholastic, 1990.

Herford, O. "A Thanksgiving Fable." In *Poetry Place Anthology*. Ed. Rosemary Alexander. New York: Scholastic, 1990.

Hoffman, A. "A New World." In *Poetry Place Anthology*. Ed. Rosemary Alexander. New York: Scholastic, 1990.

Jacobs, L. "The Mayflower." In *Poetry Place Anthology*. Ed. Rosemary Alexander. New York: Scholastic, 1990.

Livingston, M. "First Thanksgiving." In *Hand in Hand: An American History through Poetry*. Ed. Lee Bennett Hopkins. Riverdale, NJ: Simon & Schuster, 1994.

Robinson, G. "Christopher Columbus." In *Poetry Place Anthology*. Ed. Rosemary Alexander. New York: Scholastic, 1990.

Turner, F. "Signs of Thanksgiving." In *Poetry Place Anthology*. Ed. Rosemary Alexander. New York: Scholastic, 1990.

Wynne, A. "Thanksgiving Day." In *Poetry Place Anthology*. Ed. Rosemary Alexander. New York: Scholastic, 1990.

CHAPTER 2

The Old West

I Have Heard of a Land

Joyce Carol Thomas
(New York: HarperCollins, 1998)

Book Summary: The Oklahoma land runs were equally accessible to blacks and whites. This book is a tribute to the early pioneer spirit expressed through the eyes of a young black woman. The book describes what it was like to arrive in the untamed Oklahoma Territory in the late 1800s and gradually transform it into a home and a whole new way of life.

Key Concepts: Oklahoma territory, pioneers, settlers

National History Standards: 1, 2, 3, 4, 5, and 7

Activity #1: "I Live in a Land" Class Collaboration Poem

Materials for Activity #1:

- Composition paper
- Pencils
- Chart paper with example couplet written on it
- Roll of butcher paper
- Markers

Areas of Integration: Writing, oral language, poetic form

After reading and discussing *I Have Heard of a Land*, have students reflect on the ideals, freedoms, and opportunities that make living in the United States of America a special privilege.

As students brainstorm, record their responses on the chalkboard. Responses might include such things as the freedom of speech, the right to a quality public education, the celebration of various holidays, the freedom of choice, and a voice in government.

Once students have voiced their ideas, share with them the following example of a rhyming couplet displayed on chart paper:

> I live in a land where the people rule
> And all children can go to school.

Point out that a couplet consists of only two lines, and the lines rhyme. Ask students to choose one of the brainstormed ideas and create a rhyming couplet for it. Each couplet must begin with the words, "I live in a land . . ."

Once students are done, have them share their couplets in class. Following this, have them record their couplets on a large sheet to form one poem, entitled "I Live in a Land . . ." Vary the color of marker used to write each couplet to make each distinct. Hang the finished class collaboration poem in the school entryway, hallway, or in the classroom for others to enjoy.

Activity #2: A Puzzling State

Materials for Activity #2:

- 4 large sheets of poster board taped together (on back) with the outline of the state of Oklahoma drawn on it (cut outline into 24 puzzle pieces)
- Reference books or Internet access
- Crayons, markers, and/or colored pencils

Areas of Integration: Research, reading, writing, creative expression

After reading the book, discuss the Oklahoma Territory with the students and the fact that the land was open to all people, including people of color. Have students examine the page in the book just opposite the dedication page. Focus their attention on the poster that is displayed there.

Show students the large puzzle outline of the state of Oklahoma. Ask them to identify the state and ask them to share what they already know about the state. Following the discussion, tell them that they will each be assigned a piece of the puzzle. Students will choose or be assigned one of the following questions to research. Students will write the information on the puzzle piece, as well as draw a picture to accompany the fact. (If the class size exceeds 24, several children could work collaboratively on questions 16 through 20 and question 24).

1. What year was Oklahoma admitted to the Union?

2. What is Oklahoma's state flower?

3. What is Oklahoma's state bird?

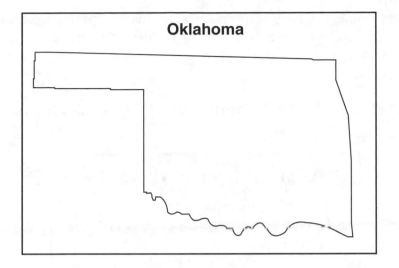

Oklahoma

4. What is Oklahoma's state animal?

5. What is Oklahoma's state tree?

6. What is Oklahoma's state beverage?

7. What is Oklahoma's state dog?

8. What is Oklahoma's state fish?

9. What is Oklahoma's state insect?

10. What is Oklahoma's nickname?

11. What is Oklahoma's state song?

12. What does Oklahoma's state seal look like?

13. What is Oklahoma's state motto?

14. What is Oklahoma's state symbol?

15. What does Oklahoma's state flag look like?

16. What are some of Oklahoma's points of interest?

17. What regional folklore exists in Oklahoma?

18. What cultural contributions has Oklahoma made?

19. What scientific contributions has Oklahoma made?

20. Which noteworthy citizens have come from Oklahoma?

21. What is the current population of Oklahoma?

22. What is the state's highest point?

23. What is the state's lowest point?

24. For which industries is Oklahoma known?

Once students are finished, have each student share his or her puzzle piece and information about Oklahoma with the class. Have them reassemble the whole puzzle on a hallway bulletin board for others to view.

Activity #3: "All about Our State" Class Book

> **Materials for Activity #3:**
> - 12″ × 18″ white drawing paper
> - Crayons, markers, and/or colored pencils
> - Reference books or Internet access
> - Paper hole punch
> - 3 ring fasteners

Areas of Integration: Reading, writing, research, oral language, creative expression

Have students learn more about their own home state by researching the answers to the questions listed in Activity #2. Explain to the class they will be creating a class book about their own state. Each person will choose or be assigned one of the 24 questions. Students will record the information that they find and illustrate it on one page of the class book.

Once students are done, have them share the information aloud with classmates. Have students organize the pages into a class book, number the pages, and create a table of contents for the book. Punch three holes down the left-hand side of the assembled book and fasten the pages together with three metal rings. The book can be displayed in the school library or classroom library for others to enjoy.

Black Cowboy, Wild Horses

Julius Lester
(New York: Dial Books, 1998)

Book Summary: This book recounts the true story of a black cowboy named Bob Lemmons. Bob is a former slave who now tracks mustangs in the Old West. He and his black stallion, Warrior, encounter wind, rain, and rattlesnakes to triumph over the mustangs and bring them into the corral.

Key Concepts: Black cowboys, the Old West

National History Standards: 5 and 6

Activity #1: Have a Book Talk

Materials for Activity #1:

- Coffee cans (1 per group)
- Construction paper, wallpaper samples, or shelf paper
- Tape and glue
- Markers or paints
- Old magazines for cutting

Areas of Integration: Creative expression, oral expression, cooperative learning

After reading and discussing *Black Cowboy, Wild Horses*, divide students into groups of three or four. Ask each group to prepare to present a book talk of the story. Have the groups cover a coffee can with construction paper or shelf paper. Students should then decorate the can with pictures, drawings, and words to represent the book. The book's title and author should be written on the can. Each student in the group must bring in at least one item to put in the can to represent something important in the story. When the cans are complete, the groups present their book talks. Have students stand in the front of the room and take turns either retelling parts of the story using the item brought in for a prop, or explaining why the item brought in was important to the story. For example, a student might bring in a plastic horse and tell how Bob's stallion, Warrior, was important to him.

Activity #2: Bio-Poems

Materials for Activity #2:

- Writing paper (1 sheet per student)

Areas of Integration: Creative writing

After reading *Black Cowboy, Wild Horses*, ask students to write bio-poems about Bob Lemmons using the following format:

Line 1: Bob's first name

Line 2: Described as . . . (four words describing Bob)

Line 3: Lover of . . . (three ideas, people, or things)

Line 4: Who challenges . . . (three ideas or things)

Line 5: Who feels . . . (three emotions)

Line 6: Who needs . . . (three ideas or things)

Source: http://projects.edtech.sandi.net/memorial/where/biopoem.htm

Line 7: Who shares . . . (three ideas or things)

Line 8: Who fears . . . (three ideas or things)

Line 9: Who would like to change . . . (one idea or thing)

Line 10: Resident of . . . (where Bob lives)

Line 11: Bob's last name

Activity #3: KWL Chart on Cowboys and Cowgirls

> **Materials for Activity #3:**
> • Chart paper
> • Books about cowboys and cowgirls

Areas of Integration: Critical thinking, reading skills, comparing and contrasting

After reading the book, make a KWL chart of cowboys and cowgirls in the Old West. After you record things that students know about cowboys and cowgirls, as well as the information they would like to find out about them, have students read other stories to learn more about cowboys and cowgirls. Other books about cowboys and cowgirls include the following:

Lazzaro, L. *Why Cowgirls Are Such Sweet Talkers.* Gretna, LA: Pelican Publishing Co., 2000.
Gibbons, G. *Yippee-Yay: A Book about Cowboys and Cowgirls.* New York: Little Brown, 1998.
Scott, A. *Cowboy Country.* Boston: Clarion, 1996.
Penner, L. *Cowboys.* New York: Grosset & Dunlap, 1996.
Pinkney, A. *Bill Pickett: Rodeo-Ridin' Cowboy.* San Diego, CA: Voyager, 1999.
Folsum, F. *Black Cowboy: The Life and Legend of George McJunkin* (The Forgotten Pioneers). Boulder, CO: Roberts Rinehart Publishers, 1992.
Time Life Books. *Cowboys of the Old West.* New York: Time Life, 1997.

Complete the KWL chart by having students describe the things that they have learned about cowboys and cowgirls from reading the books. Discuss with students the information that they found most surprising or most interesting.

Voices of the Alamo

Sherry Garland
(New York: Scholastic, 2000)

Book Summary: This book recounts the extended history of the Alamo through the voices of sixteen individuals who were involved in the unfolding of this historic drama. Individuals, from a Payaya Indian princess, to a humble padre and a Tejano rancher, to more famous figures, such as David Crockett and Santa Anna, describe different aspects of the Alamo's evolution from a mission to a monument. The sixteenth individual, a young boy of today, describes his impressions of viewing the Alamo for the first time as a tourist.

Key Concepts: The Alamo, conquistador, missions, Steven Austin, General Antonio Lopez de Santa Anna, David Crockett, James Bowie, William Barret Travis, General Sam Houston

National History Standards: 2, 3, and 4

Activity #1: Readers' Theater—Voices of the Past

> **Materials for Activity #1:**
>
> - Paper (for script writing)
> - Pencils
> - Props (brought in by students)
> - Spotlight or flashlight

Areas of Integration: Reading, writing, listening, speaking, creative dramatics

After reading *Voices of the Alamo*, have students create a readers' theater script of the book and present it to another class. Along with the sixteen characters from the book, assign several students to be narrators, production managers, lighting crewmembers, and prop coordinators. Remind students that readers' theater is not the same as a dramatic production. In readers' theater, students read from scripts and use very few props or physical gesturing.

Students might consider placing the sixteen main characters and narrators on swivel chairs in front of a dimly lit classroom. As a character reads, he or she swivels the chair around to face the audience, while a lighting crewmember illuminates the reader. Upon completion, the reader swivels the chair around, so that his or her back is away from the audience. Students can use a few simple props, such as hats, swords, and clothing items, if desired.

Students can present the readers' theater production to other classes or invite friends and family members in to watch the production.

Activity #2: Travels to Texas

> **Materials for Activity #2:**
>
> - 8½″ × 12″ white drawing paper (folded into a trifold)
> - Crayons, markers, and/or colored pencils
> - Sample travel brochures
> - Reference books or Internet access

Areas of Integration: Reading, writing, speaking, listening, creative expression

After reading *Voices of the Alamo*, ask students if any of them have ever traveled to Texas. If so, ask them to describe the places they visited in Texas and the sights they saw there.

Ask students if they know what travel brochures are. Ask them where they might find travel brochures and what travel brochures are typically used for. Ask them to tell what kinds of information are typically found in a brochure.

Following this, show students samples of brochures from different states. After examining and discussing them, sort students into pairs to create travel brochures for Texas. They will need first to research the state through reference books or the Internet. The brochure should include information on the Alamo, as well as four other areas of interest in Texas (displayed on each panel of the trifold). The front cover should display the state's name and list interesting facts about the state.

When complete, students can share their brochures in class. Brochures can be displayed, along with an informational Texas bulletin board.

Activity #3: "Who Said It and When?" Activity Game

Materials for Activity #3:

- "Who Said It and When?" game cards (provided)
- Masking tape
- Chalkboard

Areas of Integration: Reading, oral language, inference skills

After reading and discussing *Voices of the Alamo*, write the identities of the sixteen story characters on the chalkboard:

Payaya maiden	conquistador	padre
Spanish soldier	Sarah Seely DeWitt	David Crockett
Tejano rancher	Texan farmer	poor peasant
Antonio Lopez de Santa Anna	William Barret Travis	drummer
	Sam Houston	Clara Driscoll
Suzanna Dickinson		
tourist		

Next, create a time line on the board with the following key dates from the story:

1500

1542

1745

1803

1821

1830

1834

1835

February 10, 1836

February 23, 1836

March 5, 1836

March 6, 1836

April 21, 1836

1904

Today

Tell students they will be playing a game called, "Who Said It and When?" Before beginning the game, cut apart the game cards, shuffle, and assemble them in a deck with the clues and answers facing downward.

The teacher should begin by calling upon a volunteer from the class to select a clue from the deck of cards. The student then reads the clue to the class and classmates first guess who said it. After finding the correct answer to who said the phrase, the reader of the clue polls the class to find a classmate who can tell when the statement was made. If a student identifies the time correctly, he or she places it on the timeline by affixing a piece of tape to the reverse side of the card. The person who identified the date correctly becomes the next clue reader. Play continues until all cards are identified correctly and placed on the time line.

"Who Said It and When?" Activity Game

Nature provides a comfortable home. I live in the land where the buffalo roam. Who am I? When did I live? (Payaya maiden—1500)	I come from Spain with sword in hand. For God and king, I claim this land. Who am I? When did I live? (Conquistador—1542)
I built the mission with stones of white. To save what native souls I might. Who am I? When did I live? (Padre—1745)	I hide in the mission where padres used to pray. Cannons replace the crosses of yesterday. Who am I? When did I live? (Spanish soldier—1803)
Mexico is free at last! The rule of the Spanish king has finally passed. Who am I? When did I live? (Tejano rancher—1821)	Following Steven Austin's lead, I plow the soil and pull the weed. Who am I? When did I live? (Texan farmer—1830)
I am the general commanding the fights. I'll raise their taxes and take away their rights. Who am I? When did I live? (Antonio Lopez de Santa Anna—1834)	From a wedding gown I stitched a banner. Then our boys captured the mission in an impressive manner. Who am I? When did I live? (Sarah Seely DeWitt—1835)

"Who Said It and When?" Activity Game (continued)

I came from the mountains of Tennessee. I'm as rugged as a volunteer can be! Who am I? When did I live? (David Crockett—2/10/1836)	With El Presidente's men I was forced to fight, Marching through blizzards in the dead of night. Who am I? When did I live? (Poor peasant—2/23/1836)
I am the commander of the Alamo. Who drew a line in the sand below. Who am I? When did I live? (William Barret Travis—3/5/1836)	Listen for my beat to sound. I'm shivering on the cold, wet ground. Who am I? When did I live? (Drummer—3/6/1836)
I'm the wife of Almeron—my child and I tremble with fear. For my deceased husband, I shed a tear. Who am I? When did I live? (Suzanna Dickinson—3/6/1836)	I am the general who set Texas free. Remember the Alamo! Remember me! Who am I? When did I live? (Sam Houston—4/21/1836)
On the site of the mission, men build a general store. Does anyone still remember what happened here long before? Who am I? When did I live? (Clara Driscoll—1904)	I stand and I stare at the historic site. I know I'll remember the Alamo fight. Who am I? When did I live? (Tourist—today)

Related Books

Ackerman, K. *Araminta's Paint Box.* New York: Atheneum, 1990.

Alter, J. *Great Women of the Old West.* Minneapolis, MN: Compass Point, 2001.

Collins, C. *The World of Little House.* New York: Scholastic, 1996.

Cox, C. *The Forgotten Heroes: The Story of the Buffalo Soldiers.* New York: Scholastic, 1993.

Dary, D. *The Santa Fe Trail: History, Legends, and Lore.* New York: Scholastic, 2002.

Davis, K. *Don't Know Much about the Pioneers.* New York: HarperCollins, 2002.

Freedman, R. *Children of the Wild West.* New York: Scholastic, 1990.

Gerrard, R. *Wagons West.* New York: Farrar, Straus, and Giroux, 1996.

Isaacs, S. *Life on the Oregon Trail.* Chicago: Heinemann, 2000.

Kalman, B. *Bandanas, Chaps and Ten-Gallon Hats.* New York: Crabtree, 1999.

————. *The Life of a Miner.* New York: Crabtree, 2000.

————. *Women of the West.* New York: Crabtree, 2000.

Katz, W. *Black Women of the Old West.* New York: Atheneum, 1995.

Lawlor, L. *Old Grump and the True Story of a Trip West.* New York: Holiday House, 2002.

Levitin, S. *Boom Town.* New York: Orchard, 1998.

————. *Nine for California.* New York: Orchard, 1996.

McGovern, T. *African Americans in the Old West.* Chicago: Children's Press, 1998.

Moss, M. *True Heart.* New York: Scholastic, 1999.

Pelz, R. *Black Heroes of the Wild West.* Seattle, WA: Open Hand, 1990.

Rau, M. *Belle of the West: The Story of Belle Star.* Greensboro, NC: Morgan Reynolds, 2001.

Sakurai, G. *Asian Americans in the Old West.* Chicago: Children's Press, 2000.

Savage, C. *Born to Be a Cowgirl: A Spirited Ride through the Old West.* Berkeley, CA: Tricycle Press, 2001.

Schlissel, L. *Black Frontiers: A History of African American Heroes in the Old West.* New York: Aladdin, 2000.

Sperry, A. *Wagons Westward: The Old Trail to Santa Fe.* Boston: David R. Godine, 2001.

Stacey, M. *Wild West.* Hauppauge, NY: Barrons, 2001.

Stanley, J. *Hurry Freedom: African-Americans in Gold Rush California.* New York: Crown, 2000.

Sundling, C. *Explorers of the Frontier.* Edina, MN: Abdo Daughters, 2000.

Turner, A. *Red Flower Goes West.* New York: Hyperion, 1999.

Wallner, A. *Laura Ingalls Wilder.* New York: Scholastic, 1997.

Related Poetry

Benet, R., and S. Benet. "Western Wagons." In *Celebrate America in Poetry and Art.* Ed. Nora Panzer. New York: Hyperion, 1999.

Collins, B. "The Reminder." In *Poetry Place Anthology.* Ed. Rosemary Alexander. New York: Scholastic, 1990.

Fisher, Lillian M. "Pioneers." In *Hand in Hand: An American History through Poetry.* Ed. Lee Bennett Hopkins. Riverdale, NJ: Simon & Schuster, 1994.

Ford, M. L. "Frontiers." In *Poetry Place Anthology.* Ed. Rosemary Alexander. New York: Scholastic, 1990.

Hopkins, L. "Nat Love: Black Cowboy." In *Hand in Hand: An American History through Poetry.* Ed. Lee Bennett Hopkins. Riverdale, NJ: Simon & Schuster, 1994.

Hurley, W. "Home of Yesterday." In *Poetry Place Anthology*. Ed. Rosemary Alexander. New York: Scholastic, 1990.

Marshall, W. "Mehitable." In *Poetry Place Anthology*. Ed. Rosemary Alexander. New York: Scholastic, 1990.

Miller, Rachel, arr. "Cumberland Gap." In *From Sea to Shining Sea: A Treasury of American Folklore and Folk Songs*. Ed. Amy Cohn. New York: Scholastic, 1993.

Pease, J. "Candle Making." In *Poetry Place Anthology*. Ed. Rosemary Alexander. New York: Scholastic, 1990.

———. "The Covered Wagon." In *Poetry Place Anthology*. Ed. Rosemary Alexander. New York: Scholastic, 1990.

———. "Long, Long Ago." In *Poetry Place Anthology*. Ed. Rosemary Alexander. New York: Scholastic, 1990.

———. "The Stagecoach." In *Poetry Place Anthology*. Ed. Rosemary Alexander. New York: Scholastic, 1990.

Yolen, J. "A Song for Sacagawea: Lewis and Clark Expedition, 1803–1806." In *Lives: Poems about Famous Americans*. Ed. Lee Bennett Hopkins. New York: HarperCollins, 1999.

CHAPTER *3*

The American Revolution

Sybil's Night Ride

Karen Winnick
(Honesdale, PA: Boyds Mills Press, 2000)

Book Summary: In the year 1777, Sybil Ludington made a night ride through what is now Putnam County, New York, to warn residents of British invasion. This Revolutionary War tale is the true story of the brave acts of a sixteen-year-old girl.

Key Concepts: Revolutionary War, women in history

National History Standards: 1 and 4

Activity #1: If the British Had Won the Revolutionary War

Materials for Activity #1:

- Chart paper
- Writing paper (1 or 2 sheets per student)

Areas of Integration: Critical thinking, creative writing

After reading *Sybil's Night Ride*, discuss what this country might be like if the British had won the Revolutionary War. Document the differences on chart paper. Ask students to write a story detailing how their own lives might be different if the British had won. Ask for volunteers to share their stories.

Activity #2: Comparison of Sybil Ludington to Paul Revere

> **Materials for Activity #2:**
> - Character analysis handouts (1 per student)
> - Picture books about Paul Revere

Areas of Integration: Critical thinking, oral language

After reading and discussing the book, give each student a character analysis handout. Using books about Paul Revere (such as *And Then What Happened, Paul Revere?*), have students compare Sybil Ludington with Paul Revere. Students make a plus (+) to represent yes, a minus (–) to represent no, or a (+/–) to represent sometimes in the blocks for Sybil and Paul Revere. As a large group, have students discuss each character and his or her traits. Encourage students to discuss why they believe the story of Paul Revere is widely known, but the story of Sybil Ludington is virtually unknown.

Character Analysis: Sybil Ludington and Paul Revere								
	Brave	**Rode a Horse**	**Warned of British Invasion**	**Rode at Night**	**Successfully Finished Ride**	**Well Known**	**Risked Own Life**	**Met George Washington**
Sybil Ludington								
Paul Revere								

(+) = yes
(–) = no
(+/–) = sometimes

Source: Rasinski, T. & Padak, N. (2000). *Effective reading strategies.* 2nd ed. Upper Saddle River, NJ: Prentice Hall.

Activity #3: Are We Alike or Different?

> **Materials for Activity #3:**
> • Chart paper

Areas of Integration: Brainstorming, critical thinking

After reading and discussing *Sybil's Night Ride*, ask students to brainstorm qualities that describe Sybil Ludington. Then have them compare themselves with Sybil and consider the following questions:

1. How are you alike?

2. How are you different?

3. As a sixteen-year-old, do you think you would risk your life by riding forty miles alone in the dark to warn people of British invasion? Why or why not?

The American Revolution (Voices in African-American History Series)

S. Harley
(Baltimore, MD: Modern Curriculum Press, 1994)

Book Summary: During the American Revolution, some African Americans sided with the patriots; others supported the British. This book examines the role of African Americans in the war, the effect they had on its outcome, and the move to end slavery.

Key Concepts: Revolutionary War, African Americans, slavery

National History Standards: 4 and 6

Activity #1: The Relationship between the Revolutionary War and Slavery

> **Materials for Activity #1:**
> • Writing paper (1 sheet per student)

Areas of Integration: Critical thinking, written expression, oral expression

The Civil War is usually associated with slavery and issues of freedom. However, nearly 100 years prior to the Civil War, African Americans were hoping for freedom as a result of the Revolutionary War. Help students to see the relationship between the Revolutionary War, the Declaration of Independence, and African Americans' hopes for freedom by reading and discussing *The American Revolution*. Use the following questions to facilitate your discussion.

1. Why were the colonies fighting the British? What did they hope to gain?

2. How were African Americans involved in the Revolutionary War?

3. Did all African Americans support the colonies, or did some support the British? Why?

4. What were African Americans hoping for as a result of the Revolutionary War?

5. The Declaration of Independence states that "All men are created equal" and that "All people have rights to life, liberty, and the pursuit of happiness." Was this true for everyone? Why or why not?

6. How did many African Americans gain their freedom after the Revolutionary War?

Mum Bett, an African-American slave, once said, "Anytime, while I was a slave, if one minute's freedom had been offered to me, and I had been told I must die at the end of that minute, I would have taken it just to stand one minute on God's earth a free woman—I would." Ask each student to take the role of a slave, a slave owner, or an abolitionist. Have students write a letter to Mum Bett, reacting to her statement. Then place students in groups of three (each group with one slave, one slave owner, and one abolitionist) and compare their letters.

Activity #2: Shoebox Guess

Materials for Activity #2:

- Shoebox
- Items for guessing

Areas of Integration: Critical thinking, oral language

After reading and discussing *The American Revolution*, participate in a shoebox guessing game with students. Place an item that represents a person, place, or thing from the book in a shoebox. In pairs, have students create a yes or no question that they will ask to discover what is in the box. For example, you might place a picture of General George Washington in the box. Randomly select pairs of students to ask questions, allowing students to consider what the item might be. The student who guesses correctly may want to bring in the next item for guessing.

Activity #3: Rewriting History

Materials for Activity #3:

• Writing paper (1 sheet per student)

Areas of Integration: Creative writing

After reading and discussing the book, ask students to consider how the years between the Revolutionary War and the Civil War might have been different if African Americans had been granted freedom by the Declaration of Independence. Have students select one historical event that took place between 1776 and 1860 and consider how that event might have been different if African Americans had been free. Ask students to write a newspaper account of their event. Students could compile the newspaper articles into newspaper format for display in the classroom.

Come All You Brave Soldiers: Blacks in the Revolutionary War

Clinton Cox
(New York: Scholastic, 1999)

Book Summary: Thousands of African-American soldiers, both slaves and free men, fought in the Revolutionary War. *Come All You Brave Soldiers* presents the facts surrounding the men that enlisted, the battles in which they fought, and the impact of these brave men on the outcome of the Revolutionary War.

Key Concepts: Revolutionary War, African-American soldiers

National History Standards: 1 and 4

Activity #1: Decision-making Scenario: Shadrack Battle Goes to War

Materials for Activity #1:

• Scenarios: Shadrack Battle Goes to War (see box below)

Shadrack Battle Goes to War

You are Shadrack Battle, an African-American man from the state of Virginia. You have decided to join the Continental Army and you are getting ready to leave your home to enlist. You are able to carry a small pack with you, but it will hold only eight items. You must decide which of the following eight items you would find most useful during your travels. Number in the order of importance the eight items you want to take with you. Then discuss your choices with group members. Reach a group decision on the top eight things that you would take.

_____ soap	_____ flour
_____ hunting knife	_____ fishing pole
_____ wool blanket	_____ warm clothes
_____ iron pot	_____ medicine kit
_____ writing materials	_____ canteen
_____ Bible	_____ axe
_____ musket and powder	_____ vegetable seeds
_____ candles	_____ lucky coin

Areas of Integration: Decision making, collaborative learning

After reading chapter 5 in *Come All You Brave Soldiers: Blacks in the Revolutionary War*, discuss with students the numbers of African-American soldiers who enlisted during the war. Ask students to role play the life of one soldier from Virginia, Shadrack Battle. Working individually, students will rank the eight items that they would take with them to war, if they were Shadrack Battle. Then have students divide into groups of four. Each student must discuss which items he or she decided to take and then reach consensus with group members on the eight most important items.

Activity #2: Create a Bulletin Board

Materials for Activity #2:

- Bulletin board paper
- Construction paper
- Stencils for letters
- Markers
- Glue and tape
- Evaluation rubric (see box below).

Areas of Integration: Cooperative learning, creative expression, research skills, oral language

After reading and discussing the book, divide students into four groups. Assign each of the groups one of the following: main characters, plot, setting, and author. Divide a large bulletin board into four spaces. Each group must design their bulletin board space, in words and pictures, to represent their part of the book. Encourage students to use the talents of all group members. For example, some students could draw scenes, others could organize the space, and others could do research. After the bulletin board is complete, have students give an oral presentation, explaining the content of their section. When explaining the assignment, provide students with the evaluation rubric so that they understand the goals of the assignment. When evaluating each group's contribution, place a check mark on the rubric in the appropriate boxes.

Bulletin Board Evaluation Rubric			
Criteria	**6 Points**	**4 Points**	**2 Points**
Historical Accuracy	Content of bulletin board is historically accurate.	Content of bulletin board contains some historical accuracy.	Content of bulletin board contains historical inaccuracies.
Neatness and Organization	Bulletin board is very neat and exceptionally well organized.	Bulletin board is neat and organized.	Bulletin board is unorganized and messy.
Creativity	Bulletin board demonstrates exceptional creativity.	Bulletin board is somewhat creative.	Bulletin board content and design are dull and unimaginative.
Group Process	Students work together very well and work out any difficulties that may arise.	Students work together with only minor difficulties.	Students have difficulty working together and require intervention from the teacher.

Total Points = _____/24

Group Members: _____

Date: _____

Activity #3: Newspaper Articles

> ## Materials for Activity #3:
> - Writing paper (1 sheet per student)
> - Internet and library access
> - Word processor

Areas of Integration: Creative writing, research skills

After reading and discussing the book, have each student write a newspaper article about one or more characters of their choice. Have students begin by creating a catchy title. Encourage them to include historically accurate facts, but also allow for fictitious details to be added when few facts are available. Students can add to the facts in *Come All You Brave Soldiers* by conducting research in books, journals, or the Internet. Each article should answer the five newspaper questions: who, what, where, when, and why. Allow students or a volunteer adult to word process the articles into a newspaper format, focusing on the role of African Americans in the Revolutionary War. Encourage students to take turns taking the newspaper home to share it with their families.

Related Books

Aldridge, R. *Thomas Jefferson*. Mankato, MN: Bridgestone, 2001.

Arndt, U. *Fireworks, Picnics, and Flags: The Story of the Fourth of July Symbols*. New York: Clarion, 2001.

Bains, R. *James Monroe: Young Patriot*. Mahwah, NJ: Troll, 1986.

Bober, N. *Countdown to Independence: A Revolution of Ideas in England and Her American Colonies: 1760–1776*. New York: Atheneum, 2001.

Brenner, E. *If You Were There in 1776*. New York: Bradbury Press, 1994.

Buckley, G. *American Patriots: The Story of Blacks in the Military from the Revolution to Desert Storm*. New York: Crown, 2003.

Davis, B. *Black Heroes of the American Revolution*. San Diego, CA: Harcourt Brace, 1976.

Duden, J. *Betsy Ross*. Mankato, MN: Bridgestone, 2002.

Duey, K. *Mary Alice Peale: Philadelphia, 1777*. New York: Aladdin, 1996.

Furstinger, N. *The Boston Tea Party*. Mankato, MN: Bridgestone, 2002.

Gregson, S. *Benjamin Franklin*. Mankato, MN: Bridgestone, 2002.

———. *Phillis Wheatley*. Mankato, MN: Bridgestone, 2002.

Harper, J. *African Americans in the Revolutionary War*. Chanhassen, MN: Childs World, 2000.

Haskin, J. *Black Stars of Colonial Times and the Revolutionary War: African Americans Who Lived Their Dreams*. Hoboken, NJ: John Wiley & Sons, 2002.

King, D. *Revolutionary War Days: Discover the Past with Exciting Projects, Games, Activities, and Recipes*. Hoboken, NJ: John Wiley, 2001.

Leebrick, K. *The United States Constitution*. Mankato, MN: Bridgestone, 2002.

Masoff, J. *American Revolution*. New York: Scholastic, 2000.

McKinney, J. *And Then What Happened, Paul Revere?* New York: Scholastic, 1990.

Moore, K. *If You Lived at the Time of the American Revolution*. New York: Scholastic, 1998.

Murphy, J. *A Young Patriot: The American Revolution as Experienced by One Boy*. Boston: Houghton Mifflin, 1998.

Murray, S. *Eyewitness: American Revolution*. New York: DK Publishing, 2002.

Oberle, L. *The Declaration of Independence*. Mankato, MN: Bridgestone, 2002.

Payan, G. *The Marquis De Lafayette: French Hero of the American Revolution*. New York: Powerkids, 2002.

Randolph, R. *Paul Revere and the Minutemen of the American Revolution*. New York: Powerkids, 2002.

Ready, D. *The Boston Massacre*. Mankato, MN: Bridgestone, 2002.

Silcox-Jarrett, D. *Heroines of the American Revolution: America's Founding Mothers*. New York: Scholastic, 1998.

Spier, P. *We the People: The Constitution of the United States of America*. New York: Doubleday, 1987.

Wallner, A. *Betsy Ross*. New York: Scholastic, 1994.

Zeman, A., and K. Kelly. *Everything You Need to Know about American History*. New York: Scholastic, 1994.

Related Poetry

Anonymous. "Independence Bell." In *Hand in Hand: An American History through Poetry*. Ed. Lee Bennett Hopkins. Riverdale, NJ: Simon & Schuster, 1994.

Duffy, N. "America." In *Poetry Place Anthology*. Ed. Rosemary Alexander. New York: Scholastic, 1990.

———. "I Love America." In *Poetry Place Anthology*. Ed. Rosemary Alexander. New York: Scholastic, 1990.

———. "There'll Always Be America." In *Poetry Place Anthology*. Ed. Rosemary Alexander. New York: Scholastic, 1990.

Ford, M. L. "To Our Country." In *Poetry Place Anthology*. Ed. Rosemary Alexander. New York: Scholastic, 1990.

Fowler, E. "Our America." In *Poetry Place Anthology*. Ed. Rosemary Alexander. New York: Scholastic, 1990.

Hoffman, A. "Strength in Union." In *Poetry Place Anthology*. Ed. Rosemary Alexander. New York: Scholastic, 1990.

Hopkins, L. B. "John Hancock." In *Hand in Hand: An American History through Poetry*. Ed. Lee Bennett Hopkins. Riverdale, NJ: Simon & Schuster, 1994.

Leonard, A. "Fun on the Fourth of July." In *Poetry Place Anthology*. Ed. Rosemary Alexander. New York: Scholastic, 1990.

Livingston, M. C. "Paul Revere Speaks." In *Hand in Hand: An American History through Poetry*. Ed. Lee Bennett Hopkins. Riverdale, NJ: Simon & Schuster, 1994.

Longfellow, H. W. "Paul Revere's Ride." In *Hand in Hand: An American History through Poetry*. Ed. Lee Bennett Hopkins. Riverdale, NJ: Simon & Schuster, 1994.

Lowell, J. "Our Fathers Fought for Liberty." In *Celebrate America in Poetry and Art*. Ed. Nora Panzer. New York: Hyperion, 1999.

Lyon, M. "Carry On." In *Poetry Place Anthology*. Ed. Rosemary Alexander. New York: Scholastic, 1990.

Richards, L. "Molly Pitcher." In *Hand in Hand: An American History through Poetry*. Ed. Lee Bennett Hopkins. Riverdale, NJ: Simon & Schuster, 1994.

Schauffler, R., ed. *Independence Day: Its Celebrations, Spirit, and Significance As Related in Prose and Verse*. Detroit, MI: Omnigraphics, 2000.

Schimel, L. "This Bell Rings for Liberty." In *Lives: Poems about Famous Americans*. Ed. Lee Bennett Hopkins. New York: HarperCollins, 1999.

Shuckburgh, R. "Yankee Doodle." In *From Sea to Shining Sea: A Treasury of American Folklore and Folk Songs*. Ed. Amy Cohn. New York: Scholastic, 1993.

Thomson, H. "This Is America." In *Poetry Place Anthology*. Ed. Rosemary Alexander. New York: Scholastic, 1990.

Walush, E. "American Heritage." In *Poetry Place Anthology*. Ed. Rosemary Alexander. New York: Scholastic, 1990.

Whitman, W. "I Hear America Singing." In *Favorite Poetry Lesson*. Eds. Paul B. Janeczko and Judy Lyn. New York: Scholastic, 1998.

CHAPTER *4*
Slavery

Sweet Clara and the Freedom Quilt

Deborah Hopkinson
(New York: Alfred A. Knopf, 1993)

Book Summary: Clara, a young slave girl in the Big House on Home Plantation, learns how to sew from her Aunt Rachel. After saving scraps of material, Clara makes a map quilt that shows the route to the Underground Railroad and freedom. Clara eventually escapes and leaves the quilt as a guide for other slaves.

Key Concepts: Slavery, Underground Railroad

National History Standards: 1, 4, and 7

Activity #1: Class Freedom Quilt

> **Materials for Activity #1:**
> - Various colors of drawing paper (1 sheet per student)
> - Markers
> - Large (gallon-size) zipper-lock plastic bags (1 per student)
> - Colored craft tape

Areas of Integration: Artistic and creative expression

After reading *Sweet Clara and the Freedom Quilt*, ask students to think about the word "freedom." Ask students which people throughout history and symbols come to mind when they hear this word.

Give each student a piece of drawing paper that is the same size as the gallon-size, zipper-lock plastic bag. Using colored markers, ask them to draw what they think of when they hear the word "freedom"; for example, a US flag, the bald eagle, Abraham Lincoln, and Martin Luther King, Jr. When drawings are complete, place each in a zipper-lock plastic bag. Lay plastic bags on the floor to form a square or rectangle shape. Adhere edges of the bags together with colored craft tape to form a class freedom quilt. Do not tape the individual bags shut so that the contents can be changed from time to time.

Display the finished quilt in the classroom for all to enjoy.

Activity #2: Journey to Freedom

Materials for Activity #2:

- Writing paper
- Pencils
- Props for dramatic skits

Areas of Integration: Creative writing, oral language, creative dramatics

After completing the reading of *Sweet Clara and the Freedom Quilt*, have students continue the storyline of Clara's journey to freedom. Invite students to complete one of the following activities:

1. Write the next section of the book that tells what happened to Clara after she covered Aunt Rachel with the quilt and departed on her journey to freedom.

2. Write several journal or diary entries from Clara's point of view while on her journey to freedom or after arriving in Canada.

3. Develop a script for a dramatic skit dealing with Clara's journey to freedom. Perform it for the class.

Encourage students to share their freedom projects with the class when the work is complete.

Activity #3: Make a Map

Materials for Activity #3:

- Drawing paper
- Samples of different kinds of maps
- Colored pencils

Areas of Integration: Map skills, creative thinking, problem solving, measuring, cooperative learning

After reading the book, discuss how difficult it must have been for Clara to create a map of somewhere she had never been by simply listening to the conversations of others. Show students examples of different kinds of maps and discuss the usefulness of them.

In small groups, have students create simple maps/floor plans of different areas of the school, such as the cafeteria, gymnasium, library, or office. Have them include appropriate symbols, a legend, and a scale. After the maps are complete, groups can exchange them and check the accuracy.

Activity #4: Acrostic Freedom Poems

Materials for Activity #4:
- Sample of an acrostic poem
- Chart paper
- Composition paper
- Pencils

Areas of Integration: Reading, writing, creative thinking, oral language

After reading the book, write the word "freedom" on a large sheet of chart paper. Ask students to brainstorm words, phrases, people, places, and events that come to mind when they think of the concept of freedom. Ask them to write their ideas on the chart paper beneath the word. Following this, show students an example of an acrostic poem. Discuss the format for composing an acrostic poem. Explain that a word or phrase, such as freedom, is written, letter by letter, in a vertical manner down the left-hand side of the paper. The author of the poem then creates a poem about the concept. The first letter of each line must be the first letter of the word or phase that begins that line.

Ask students to write an original acrostic poem using one or more of the words or phrases brainstormed at the beginning of the period. After they have completed the assignment, students can share their poems in class. Poems can be collected and assembled into a class collaboration book. Copies of the poem booklet can be copied and distributed to students for sharing at home.

Source: Hennings, D. (2002). *Communication in action: Teaching literature-based language Arts.* Boston, MA: Houghton-Mifflin Company.

Activity #5: Follow the Stars: Singing the Route to Freedom

Materials for Activity #5:
- Book: *Follow the Drinking Gourd* by Jeanette Winter
- Song: "Follow the Drinking Gourd," written on large chart paper

Areas of Integration: Reading, music, analytical thinking

Follow the Drinking Gourd tells the story of a peg-legged sailor who helps slaves during their escape on the Underground Railroad. Peg Leg Joe teaches the slaves a song about the drinking gourd, which is another name for the Big Dipper. People are able to make their escape to freedom by following the song's directions.

After reading the book, have students sing the song "Follow the Drinking Gourd," which is found at the end of the book. Discuss how it helped the slaves in their quest for freedom. Have students discuss the similarity between the creativity of Clara's quilt and Peg-Leg Joe's song. Brainstorm other creative ways, beside sewing and song, which people could have used to pass along information to the escaping slaves.

If You Traveled on the Underground Railroad

E. Levine and L. Johnson
(New York: Scholastic, 1993)

Book Summary: This informational picture book provides a detailed account of the Underground Railroad and its operation. Students can discover how the Underground Railroad got its name, what dangers the slaves faced, who worked on the Underground Railroad, and what happened when slaves got caught.

Key Concepts: Underground Railroad, slavery

National History Standards: 1, 4, and 5

Activity #1: Heroes of the Underground Railroad

> **Materials for Activity #1:**
>
> • Chart paper
> • Library and Internet resources

Areas of Integration: Critical thinking, research skills, oral language

1. After reading and discussing *If You Traveled on the Underground Railroad*, ask students to list the qualities of a hero. List these qualities on chart paper or the blackboard. Have students name some of their modern-day heroes and identify the qualities on the list that these individuals possess.

2. Ask students to identify heroes of the Underground Railroad. Harriet Tubman, Thomas Garrett, Harriet Beecher Stowe, and William Lloyd Garrison are discussed

in the book, and students might also consider William Still, Frederick Douglass, and Susan B. Anthony. Have students research and identify, through additional reading and website information, the heroic qualities possessed by these individuals and add those qualities to the list. Discuss with students the conditions in which slaves lived and the dangers they faced when trying to escape. Ask students if they believe that slaves could have successfully made it through the Underground Railroad without the help of these heroes.

3. In small groups, ask students to discuss whether they think they would have worked on the Underground Railroad to help slaves escape. Have students state their decisions and then list the pros and cons of their decisions on the handout provided (see handout). Remind them to consider the dangers to themselves and their families. Students should read about the Fugitive Slave Act of 1850 before making their decisions. In the large group, allow students to discuss the reasons behind their decisions and the problems they faced in making them.

Would I Have Worked on the Underground Railroad?

My Decision:

_____

_____

_____

Pros   *Cons*

Activity #2: A Simulation of the Underground Railroad

Materials for Activity #2:

- Signs that say, "I'm a runaway slave on the Underground Railroad. I'm heading North to freedom." (1 per student)
- Freedom cards (1 per student)
- Signs for heroes and foes

Areas of Integration: Problem solving, dramatic expression

After reading and discussing the book, allow students to experience the idea of the Underground Railroad through a simulation. Each student will play the role of a slave who is trying to gain freedom through the Underground Railroad. They each have a sign hanging around their neck that says, "I'm a runaway slave on the Underground Railroad. I'm heading North to freedom." Teachers and staff members in the school are given either "hero" or "foe" signs. Students should leave the classroom at five- to ten-minute intervals with their freedom cards and attempt to make their way to "freedom" in the gym. Each "slave" must have five "heroes" initial their card before entering the gym and receiving their freedom. If two "foes" initial their card, students must return to slavery in the classroom. Discuss with students how they felt during the activity and ask them to relate their feelings to how the slaves must have felt during their escape.

Activity #3: How Technology Might Have Changed the Underground Railroad

---

Materials for Activity #3:

• Writing paper

Areas of Integration: Critical thinking, problem solving

After reading and discussing *If You Traveled on the Underground Railroad*, divide students into small groups. Have students discuss how today's technology (computers, Internet access, transportation, telephones, etc.) might have changed the slaves' travel north on the Underground Railroad. Have students document on paper the benefits to the slaves and the benefits to those who were trying to capture them. Have each group reach consensus on the one type of technology that they believe would have had the greatest impact on the Underground Railroad. Have each group discuss this technology and explain its benefits to the class.

Ebony Sea

Irene Smalls
(Stamford: CT: Longmeadow Press, 1995)

Book Summary: This book describes the tragic story of proud Africans, known as Ebos, who were torn from their native African homeland and doomed to a life of inhumane servitude in America. Based on a historical event, the book recounts how entire families chose a dignified death in the waters off the coast of Georgia over an unbearable life of slavery. The somber tale of the day the sea turned ebony continues to echo today through the spirit of an old black storyteller named Benriver.

Agree or Disagree? Why?

AGREE

DISAGREE

1. Example: Dying for
   one's beliefs
   is an honorable act.

2.

1. Example: Suicide
   is never right.

2.

STATEMENT

CONSIDER THE FOLLOWING
STATEMENT. RELATE THE
STATEMENT TO EVENTS IN
EBONY SEA, AS WELL AS
OTHER SIMILAR EVENTS IN
HISTORY.

It is morally and ethically right
to die for a cause in which you
believe.

Key Concepts: Ebos, slavery, slave ships, plantations, cabin boy, human dignity, Middle Passage, and slave masters

National History Standards: 4, 5, and 7

Activity #1: Agree or Disagree? Why?

> **Materials for Activity #1:**
> - Agree or Disagree? Why? handout

Areas of Integration: Oral language, listening, consensus building, divergent thinking

After reading *Ebony Sea*, divide students into groups of four. Give each group a copy of the Agree or Disagree? Why? handout. Focus their attention on the statement in the middle of the handout. Direct them to discuss the issue related to the book and brainstorm possible reasons why they might agree with the statement. These should be recorded in the "Agree" section of the handout. Following this, ask them to brainstorm possible reasons for disagreeing with the statement and list these in the "Disagree" section.

When the groups have finished, combine two groups of four to discuss their combined thoughts. After the discussion is complete, ask the newly formed group of eight students to reach a consensus on whether they agree or disagree with the original statement based upon the ideas and discussions that ensued in the combined group session.

Have each group present their final thoughts to the entire class and compare differences of opinion within the classroom.

Activity #2: *Ebony Sea* Story Scroll

> **Materials for Activity #2:**
> - White roll paper (cut into 18-inch lengths) (1 per student)
> - 2 dowel rods cut to the width of the roll paper
> - Colored chalk
> - Drawing pencils
> - Transparent tape

Areas of Integration: Creative and artistic expression, sequencing, cooperative group work

After reading *Ebony Sea*, discuss the sequence of story events in the story and list these on the chalkboard. Divide students into pairs and have each pair select a scene to illustrate on white roll paper. Also, ask them to create titles for their scenes and place them at the bottom of their illustrations.

When students have finished illustrating and writing titles, have them reassemble the story illustrations into the correct sequence of events. Join the pictures together into a long scroll by taping them together on the backside with transparent tape. Ask for volunteers to create a title section and illustrators' page to attach to the beginning of the scroll. Affix wooden dowel rods to the beginning and end of the story scroll.

Students can collectively retell the story of the *Ebony Sea* to an audience by sharing their story scroll.

Activity #3: My Own Oral History

Materials for Activity #3:

• Personal photographs (brought in by students)

Areas of Integration: Speaking, listening, conversational skills

After reading *Ebony Sea*, discuss with students the role of the storyteller, Benriver, in the story. Explain to students that every individual possesses a history and that many people are not even aware of the details that relate to their early lives. To get students thinking, ask questions such as the following:

1. Do you know where you were born?

2. Do you know the time of day or night when you were born?

3. Who was present at your birth?

4. Who decided upon your name?

5. Were you named after anybody in particular?

6. What was the weather like the day on which you were born?

7. Who came to see you while you were in the hospital?

8. What was your favorite toy as a young child?

9. What was/were your first word(s)?

10. What was your first outing after you arrived home?

11. When did you take your first steps?

12. What were your favorite and least favorite foods when you were a baby?

Tell students that they will be talking with parents, grandparents, siblings, and other relatives to discover more about their own early histories. They are to find out as much as they can about their early histories and be prepared to share them in class. Encourage them to bring photographs of themselves at different ages to share while they are relating their own personal oral histories. Students might even sign up in advance for a date on which they will invite parents or other relatives to come to class to help share their oral histories with the class.

Related Books

Diouf, S. *Growing Up in Slavery*. Brookfield, CT: Millbrook Press, 2001.

Edwards, P. *Barefoot: Escape on the Underground Railroad*. New York: HarperCollins, 1999.

Fradin, D. *Bound for the North Star: True Stories of Fugitive Slaves*. New York: Clarion, 2000.

Fremon, D. *The Jim Crow Laws and Racism in American History*. Berkeley Heights, NJ: Enslow, 2000.

Gorrell, G. *North Star to Freedom: The Story of the Underground Railroad*. New York: Delacorte, 2000.

Hahn, M. *Promises to the Dead*. New York: HarperTrophy, 2002.

Hamilton, V. *Many Thousand Gone: African Americans from Slavery to Freedom*. New York: Knopf, 2002.

Haskins, J. *Get on Board: The Story of the Underground Railroad*. New York: Scholastic, 1993.

Hopkinson, D. *Under the Quilt of Night*. New York: Atheneum, 2002.

Johnson, D. *Seminole Diary: Remembrances of a Slave*. Riverside, NJ: Macmillan, 1994.

Lester, J. *From Slave Ship to Freedom Road*. New York: Puffin, 1998.

———. *To Be a Slave*. New York: Scholastic, 1968.

Levitin, S. *Dream Freedom*. San Diego, CA: Silver Whistle, 2000.

Lutz, N. *Frederick Douglass: Abolitionist and Author*. Broomall, PA: Chelsea House, 2001.

McGill, A. *In the Hollow of Your Hand*. Boston: Houghton Mifflin, 2000.

McGovern, A. *Wanted Dead or Alive: The True Story of Harriet Tubman*. New York: Scholastic, 1991.

McKissack, P. *Days of Jubilee: The End of Slavery in the United States*. New York: Scholastic, 2002.

Monroe, J. *The Underground Railroad Bringing Slaves North to Freedom*. Mankato, MN: Bridgestone, 2002.

Mullen, K. *The Story of Harriet Tubman, Conductor of the Underground Railroad*. New York: Dell, 1991.

Pearsall, S. *Trouble Don't Last*. New York: Knopf, 2002.

Pinkney, A. *Dear Benjamin Banneker*. San Diego, CA: Harcourt Brace, 1994.

Riehecky, J. *The Emancipation Proclamation: The Abolition of Slavery*. Chicago: Heinemann Library, 2002.

Sawyer, K. *Freedom Calls: Journal of a Slave Girl*. Shippensburg, PA: White Mane, 2001.

Sterling, D. *Freedom Train: The Story of Harriet Tubman*. New York: Scholastic, 1987.

Turner, A., and R. Himler. *Nettie's Trip South*. New York: Scholastic, 1987.

Vaughan, M. *The Secret to Freedom*. New York: Lee & Low, 2001.

Williams, C. *The Underground Railroad (Journey to Freedom)*. Chanhassen, MN: Childs World, 2001.

Williams, J. *African Americans in the Colony*. Minneapolis, MN: Compass Point Books, 2002.

Winter, J. *Follow the Drinking Gourd*. New York: Trumpet, 1998.

Wright, C. *Journey to Freedom: A Story of the Underground Railroad*. New York: Holiday House, 1999.

Related Poetry

Anonymous. "Harriet Tubman." In *Hand in Hand: An American History through Poetry*. Ed. Lee Bennett Hopkins. Riverdale, NJ: Simon & Schuster, 1994.

Greenfield, E. "Harriet Tubman." In *From Sea to Shining Sea: A Treasury of American Folklore and Folk Songs*. Ed. Amy Cohn. New York: Scholastic, 1993.

McLoughland, B. "The Whippoorwill Calls." In *Lives: Poems about Famous Americans*. Ed. Lee Bennett Hopkins. New York: HarperCollins, 1999.

Raph, T. "Go Down Moses." In *From Sea to Shining Sea: A Treasury of American Folklore and Folk Songs*. Ed. Amy Cohn. New York: Scholastic, 1993.

Rappaport, D. *No More!: Stories and Songs of Slave Resistance*. Cambridge, MA: Candlewick Press, 2002.

Whitman, W. "Song of Myself." In *Hand in Hand: An American History through Poetry*. Ed. Lee Bennett Hopkins. Riverdale, NJ: Simon & Schuster, 1994.

CHAPTER 5

Freedom Fighters

The Story of Ruby Bridges

Robert Coles
(New York: Scholastic, 1995)

Book Summary: This is the story of a six-year-old black child who was the first student to attend an all-white elementary school. Ruby had to be escorted to school by federal marshals, and she faced angry mobs of people every morning as she entered the building. Ruby was brave and compassionate, and instead of being angry with these people, she prayed for them.

Key Concepts: Racism, desegregation

National History Standard: 4

Activity #1: Discussion of "The Problem We All Live With"

> **Materials for Activity #1:**
> - *Through My Eyes* by Ruby Bridges (Scholastic, 1999)

Areas of Integration: Oral language, problem solving

After reading and discussing *The Story of Ruby Bridges*, introduce the book *Through My Eyes*, the autobiography of Ruby Bridges. In *Through My Eyes*, there is a picture of Ruby in a Norman Rockwell painting, "The Problem We All Live With." Show this picture to the students and ask them to discuss why Rockwell gave the painting that title. Discuss the following topics:

1. Do we still live with this problem?

2. Are we as a nation making progress toward resolving this problem?

3. What can we as students and teachers do to resolve this problem?

Encourage students to make changes in their homes, school, and community to help rid our country of racism.

Activity #2: Pen Pal Project

Materials for Activity #2:
- Writing paper, envelopes, and stamps
- E-mail access

Areas of Integration: Writing, technology

After reading the book, discuss with students the advantages of getting to know children who are different from them. Explain that prejudice often comes from ignorance, or not knowing enough about the lives and experiences of people who are different. Begin a pen pal exchange or e-mail dialogue between the students in your classroom and students of the same grade in a school that is very different from yours. Students might be different in racial or ethnic background, socioeconomic status, or size of community. As students get to know one another, hold ongoing discussions about how they are alike and different from their pen pals.

Activity #3: Five Senses Poem

Materials for Activity #3:
- Writing paper (1 sheet per student)

Areas of Integration: Creative writing

After reading and discussing *The Story of Ruby Bridges*, have students brainstorm some of the emotions that Ruby might have felt during her experiences at school. Record the emotions on chart paper. Ask students to select one emotion from the list and write a five-senses poem. Use the following format:

Line 1: Associate the emotion with a color

Line 2: Tell how the emotion sounds

Line 3: Tell how the emotion feels

Line 4: Tell how the emotion smells

Line 5: Tell how the emotion tastes

Example:

Loneliness is blue.

It sounds like an empty seashell.

It feels like a stomach ache.

It smells like a deserted house.

It tastes like toothpaste.

Source: http://ericir.syr.edu/Virtual/Lessons/Health/Body_Systems_and_Senses/BSS0009.html

A Picture Book of Rosa Parks

David Adler
(New York: Scholastic, 1993)

Book Summary: On December 1, 1955, in Montgomery, Alabama, a courageous woman named Rosa Parks, refused to give up her seat on the bus to a white passenger. Her actions that day helped change the course of history for the following generations.

Key Concepts: Segregation, discrimination, Civil Rights movement, Jim Crow laws

National History Standards: 2, 4, and 7

Activity #1: The Life and Times of Rosa Parks: A Class Collaboration Book

Materials for Activity #1:

- White drawing paper
- Rosa Parks class collaboration book page headers (see box below)
- Hole punch
- 3 metal rings (for binding book)

Rosa Parks Class Collaboration Book Page Headers

February 4, 1913: Rosa McCauley Is Born

1915: Brother, Sylvester, Is Born

1924: Rosa Continues Studies in Montgomery, Alabama

1929: Rosa Leaves School Due to Family Illness

1931: Rosa Meets Raymond Parks

December 1932: Rosa Marries Raymond Parks

1933: Rosa Finishes High School

Early 1940s: Rosa Joins National Association for the Advancement of Colored People (NAACP)

1943: Rosa Leaves Bus after Being Asked to Use Back Door

December 1, 1955: Rosa Is Arrested for Not Giving Up Her Seat on the Bus

December 5, 1955: Rosa Is Found Guilty of Breaking Segregation Laws, and Bus Boycott Begins

November 13, 1956: US Supreme Court Rules Segregation on Public Buses Is Against the Law

December 21, 1956: Bus Boycott Ends in Montgomery, Alabama

1957: Rosa Moves to Detroit, Michigan, after Receiving Threatening Phone Calls

1977: Raymond Parks Dies

1979: Rosa's Mother Dies

1987: Rosa Founds the Rosa and Raymond Parks Institute for Self-Development and Is Awarded the Medal of Freedom

Areas of Integration: Reading, writing, artistic expression

After reading *A Picture Book of Rosa Parks*, ask students to create their own class collaboration picture book that highlights the events in Rosa Parks' life. Assign students in pairs, or as individuals, to draw and write about one of the events in Rosa Parks' life. Place each page header at the top of a piece of white drawing paper. Beneath the headers, students will draw pictures depicting the event. Below the pictures, ask students to write several sentences that more fully describe the event depicted.

After adding a student-created cover page and authors'/illustrators' page, have students arrange the book in chronological order, punch three holes down the left side of the book, and bind with three metal rings. Donate the book to the school library for display.

Activity #2: Jim Crow Laws

Materials for Activity #2:

- Jim Crow laws (see box)
- Shoeboxes (1 per student)
- Markers
- Yarn
- Construction paper
- Glue
- Various other art supplies
- Index cards (1 per student)

Areas of Integration: Creative and artistic expression, oral language

Between the 1880s and the 1960s, many US states adhered to the Jim Crow laws. These laws enforced segregation and punished people for associating with people of other races.

Distribute copies of the Jim Crow laws to students. As a class, read through them and discuss the grave injustice fostered by these laws. Following this, have students create shoebox scenes depicting instances of segregation that actually existed in the South during this time period. Students can use the Jim Crow laws for ideas of possible scenarios and settings (for example, buses, hospitals, railroads, restaurants, pools, restrooms, parks, and schools). Students should write down the Jim Crow law depicted by the diorama and display it with their scenes.

When complete, display the shoebox scenes in the hallway for others to view.

Jim Crow Laws

(1880–1960s)

Here is a sampling of laws from various states:

Nurses—No person or corporation shall require any white female nurse to nurse in wards or rooms in hospitals, either public or private, in which Negro men are placed. Alabama

Buses—All passenger stations in this state operated by any motor transportation company shall have separate waiting rooms or space and separate ticket windows for the white and colored races. Alabama

Railroads—The conductor of each passenger train is authorized and required to assign each passenger to the car or the division of the car, when it is divided by a partition, designated for the race to which such passenger belongs. Alabama

Restaurants—It shall be unlawful to conduct a restaurant or other place for the serving of food in the city, at which white and colored people are served in the same room, unless such white and colored persons are effectually separated by a solid partition extending from the floor upward to a distance of seven feet or higher, and unless a separate entrance from the street is provided for each compartment. Alabama

Pool and Billiard Rooms—It shall be unlawful for a Negro and white person to play together or in company with each other at any game of pool or billiards. Alabama

Toilet Facilities, Male—Every employer of white or Negro males shall provide for such white or Negro males reasonably accessible and separate toilet facilities. Alabama

Intermarriage—The marriage of a person of Caucasian blood with a Negro, Mongolian, Malay, or Hindu shall be null and void. Arizona

Intermarriage—All marriages between a white person and a Negro, or between a white person and a person of Negro descent to the fourth generation inclusive, are hereby forever prohibited. Florida

Cohabitation—Any Negro man and white woman, or any white man and Negro woman, who are not married to each other, who shall habitually live in and occupy in the nighttime the same room shall each be punished by imprisonment not exceeding twelve (12) months, or by fine not exceeding five hundred ($500.00) dollars. Florida

Education—The schools for white children and the schools for Negro children shall be conducted separately. Florida

Juvenile Delinquents—There shall be separate buildings, not nearer than one-fourth mile to each other, one for white boys and one for Negro boys. White boys and Negro boys shall not, in any manner, be associated together or work together. Florida

Mental Hospitals—The Board of Control shall see that proper and distinct apartments are arranged for said patients, so that in no case shall Negroes and white persons be together. Georgia

Intermarriage—It shall be unlawful for a white person to marry anyone except a white person. Any marriage in violation of this section shall be void. Georgia

Jim Crow Laws (continued)

Barbers—No colored barber shall serve as a barber [to] white women or girls. Georgia

Burial—The officer in charge shall not bury, or allow to be buried, any colored persons upon ground set apart or used for the burial of white persons. Georgia

Restaurants—All persons licensed to conduct a restaurant, shall serve either white people exclusively or colored people exclusively and shall not sell to the two races within the same room or serve the two races anywhere under the same license. Georgia

Amateur Baseball—It shall be unlawful for any amateur white baseball team to play baseball on any vacant lot or baseball diamond within two blocks of a playground devoted to the Negro race, and it shall be unlawful for any amateur colored baseball team to play baseball in any vacant lot or baseball diamond within two blocks of any playground devoted to the white race. Georgia

Parks—It shall be unlawful for colored people to frequent any park owned or maintained by the city for the benefit, use and enjoyment of white persons . . . and unlawful for any white person to frequent any park owned or maintained by the city for the use and benefit of colored persons. Georgia

Wine and Beer—All persons licensed to conduct the business of selling beer or wine . . . shall serve either white people exclusively or colored people exclusively and shall not sell to the two races within the same room at any time. Georgia

Reform Schools—The children of white and colored races committed to the houses of reform shall be kept entirely separate from each other. Kentucky

Circus Tickets—All circuses, shows, and tent exhibitions, to which the attendance of . . . more than one race is invited or expected to attend shall provide for the convenience of its patrons not less than two ticket offices with individual ticket sellers, and not less than two entrances to the said performance, with individual ticket takers and receivers, and in the case of outside or tent performances, the said ticket offices shall not be less than twenty-five (25) feet apart. Louisiana

Housing—Any person . . . who shall rent any part of any such building to a Negro person or a Negro family when such building is already in whole or in part in occupancy by a white person or white family, vice versa when the building is in occupancy by a Negro person or Negro family, shall be guilty of a misdemeanor and on conviction thereof shall be punished by a fine of not less than or twenty-five ($25.00) nor more than one hundred ($100.00) dollars or be imprisoned not less than 10, or more than 60 days, or both such fine and imprisonment in the discretion of the court. Louisiana

The Blind—The board of trustees shall . . . maintain a separate building . . . on separate ground for the admission, care, instruction, and support of all blind persons of the colored or black race. Louisiana

Intermarriage—All marriages between a white person and a Negro, or between a white person and a person of Negro descent, to the third generation, inclusive, or between a white person and a member of the Malay race; or between the Negro and a member of the Malay race; or between a person of Negro descent, to the third generation, inclusive, and a member of the Malay race, are forever prohibited, and shall be void. Maryland

Railroads—All railroad companies and corporations, and all persons running or operating cars or coaches by steam on any railroad line or track in the State of Maryland, for the transportation of passengers, are hereby required to provide separate cars or coaches for the travel and transportation of the white and colored passengers. Maryland

Jim Crow Laws (continued)

Education—Separate schools shall be maintained for the children of the white and colored races. Mississippi

Promotion of Equality—Any person . . . who shall be guilty of printing, publishing or circulating printed, typewritten or written matter urging or presenting for public acceptance or general information, arguments or suggestions in favor of social equality or of intermarriage between whites and Negroes, shall be guilty of a misdemeanor and subject to fine or not exceeding five hundred (500.00) dollars or imprisonment not exceeding six (6) months or both. Mississippi

Intermarriage—The marriage of a white person with a Negro or mulatto or person, who shall have one-eighth or more of Negro blood, shall be unlawful and void. Mississippi

Hospital Entrances—There shall be maintained by the governing authorities of every hospital maintained by the state for treatment of white and colored patients separate entrances for white and colored patients and visitors, and such entrances shall be used by the race only for which they are prepared. Mississippi

Prisons—The warden shall see that the white convicts shall have separate apartments for both eating and sleeping from the Negro convicts. Mississippi

Education—Separate free schools shall be established for the education of children of African descent; and it shall be unlawful for any colored child to attend any white school, or any white child to attend a colored school. Missouri

Intermarriage—All marriages between . . . white persons and Negroes or white persons and Mongolians . . . are prohibited and declared absolutely void. . . . No person having one-eighth part or more of Negro blood shall be permitted to marry any white person, nor shall any white person be permitted to marry any Negro or person having one-eighth part or more of Negro blood. Missouri

Education—Separate rooms [shall] be provided for the teaching of pupils of African descent, and [when] said rooms are so provided, such pupils may not be admitted to the school rooms occupied and used by pupils of Caucasian or other descent. New Mexico

Textbooks—Books shall not be interchangeable between the white and colored schools, but shall continue to be used by the race first using them. North Carolina

Libraries—The state librarian is directed to fit up and maintain a separate place for the use of the colored people who may come to the library for the purpose of reading books or periodicals. North Carolina

Militia—The white and colored militia shall be separately enrolled, and shall never be compelled to serve in the same organization. No organization of colored troops shall be permitted where white troops are available, and while white permitted to be organized, colored troops shall be under the command of white officers. North Carolina

Transportation—The . . . Utilities Commission . . . is empowered and directed to require the establishment of separate waiting rooms at all stations for the white and colored races. North Carolina

Teaching—Any instructor who shall teach in any school, college or institution where members of the white and colored race are received and enrolled as pupils for instruction shall be deemed guilty of a misdemeanor, and upon conviction thereof, shall be fined in any sum not less than ten dollars ($10.00) nor more than fifty dollars ($50.00) for each offense. Oklahoma

Jim Crow Laws (continued)

Fishing, Boating, and Bathing—The [Conservation] Commission shall have the right to make segregation of the white and colored races as to the exercise of rights of fishing, boating and bathing. Oklahoma

Mining—The baths and lockers for the Negroes shall be separate from the white race, but may be in the same building. Oklahoma

Telephone Booths—The Corporation Commission is hereby vested with power and authority to require telephone companies . . . to maintain separate booths for white and colored patrons when there is a demand for such separate booths. That the Corporation Commission shall determine the necessity for said separate booths only upon complaint of the people in the town and vicinity to be served after due hearing as now provided by law in other complaints filed with the Corporation Commission. Oklahoma

Lunch Counters—No persons, firms, or corporations, who or which furnish meals to passengers at station restaurants or station eating houses, in times limited by common carriers of said passengers, shall furnish said meals to white and colored passengers in the same room, or at the same table, or at the same counter. South Carolina

Child Custody—It shall be unlawful for any parent, relative, or other white person in this State, having the control or custody of any white child, by right of guardianship, natural or acquired, or otherwise, to dispose of, give or surrender such white child permanently into the custody, control, maintenance, or support, of a Negro. South Carolina

Libraries—Any white person of such county may use the county free library under the rules and regulations prescribed by the commissioner's court and may be entitled to all the privileges thereof. Said court shall make proper provision for the Negroes of said county to be served through a separate branch or branches of the county free library, which shall be administered by [a] custodian of the Negro race under the supervision of the county librarian. Texas

Education—[The County Board of Education] shall provide schools of two kinds; those for white children and those for colored children. Texas

Theaters—Every person . . . operating . . . any public hall, theatre, opera house, motion picture show or any place of public entertainment or public assemblage which is attended by both white and colored persons, shall separate the white race and the colored race and shall set apart and designate . . . certain seats therein to be occupied by white persons and a portion thereof, or certain seats therein, to be occupied by colored persons. Virginia

Railroads—The conductors or managers on all such railroads shall have power, and are hereby required, to assign to each white or colored passenger his or her respective car, coach or compartment. If the passenger fails to disclose his race, the conductor and managers, acting in good faith, shall be the sole judges of his race. Virginia

Intermarriage—All marriages of white persons with Negroes, Mulattos, Mongolians, or Malaya hereafter contracted in the State of Wyoming are and shall be illegal and void. Wyoming

Source: http://afroamhistory.about.com/gi/dynamic/offsite.htm?site=http%3A%2F%2Fwww.udayton.edu2F%7Erace%2FO2rights%2Fjcrow02.htm

Activity #3: Newscast from the Past

> **Materials for Activity #3:**
> - Composition paper
> - Simple student-created props
> - Video camera and videotape

Areas of Integration: Reading, writing, oral expression, creative dramatics

After reading about Rosa Parks, have students create a newscast from the past. Ask them to imagine being a news reporter from the South whose job it is to interview book characters shortly after the December 1, 1955 incident in which Rosa refused to surrender her bus seat to a white passenger. Possible characters to interview include Rosa Parks, Leona and James McCauley (Rosa's parents), Sylvester McCauley (Rosa's brother), Raymond Parks (Rosa's husband), James Blake (bus driver), passengers on the bus, the arresting officer, and Dr. Martin Luther King, Jr.

Students can be assigned to small groups to complete the project. After having been assigned a person to interview, students should construct interview questions and appropriate responses. Students can decide who will be the interviewer and who will be the book character being interviewed.

Encourage students to create simple props to enhance the production. Videotape the entire newscast so that students can view it in its entirety.

As an extension activity, share with students *"Interview with Rosa Parks,"* conducted in 1997, which can be found at http://teacher.scholastic.com/rosa/rosatran.htm.

Source: Kornfield, J. (1995). Historical fiction and multicultural education in a World War II unit. In C. Bennet, ed., *Comprehensive multicultural education: Theory and practice*. 3rd ed. Boston: Allyn & Bacon.

If You Lived at the Time of Martin Luther King

Ellen Levine
(New York: Scholastic, 1994)

Book Summary: *If You Lived at the Time of Martin Luther King* describes King's life and his struggles for equality in a white man's world.

Key Concepts: Segregation, protest, boycott, Civil Rights movement, equality

National History Standards: 2 and 4

Activity #1: Mapping the Life and Times of Martin Luther King

Materials for Activity #1:

- Chart paper
- Colored markers
- Large wall map of the United States
- Pushpins
- Yarn
- 5″ × 7″ unlined index cards

Areas of Integration: Listening comprehension, geography, writing

Before reading *If You Lived at the Time of Martin Luther King*, ask students to listen for key events and places in the life of Martin Luther King. While reading, have students record a chronology of important events and places on chart paper. After reading, review the chronology and locate important places in the life of King on a large wall map of the United States. Have students insert pushpins at the site of key places. They can write a brief description of the location's significance on an index card. Attach yarn to each pushpin, and cut the yarn so that it is long enough to reach the map's perimeter. Place the index cards at the end of the yarn strand that matches the corresponding location.

Activity #2: Joining Hands for Diversity

Materials for Activity #2:

- White construction paper (1 per student)
- Multicultural colored paints or crayons
- Scissors
- Pencils

Areas of Integration: Artistic expression, writing, oral language

After discussing the book, discuss the meaning and values of diversity. Ask students to discuss

1. How are people similar?

2. How are they different?

On a piece of white construction paper, have students trace their hands and cut them out. Each student will use multicultural colored paints or crayons to shade the hand cutouts to match their own skin color. This will require some blending of colors.

After the paints are dry or coloring is complete, have students write how they are similar to other classmates on one hand and how they are different on the other. Collect the hand cutouts and connect them together, like a large chain. Display them on the walls of the classroom.

Activity #3: Diversity Garden

Materials for Activity #3:

- Flower seeds of various shapes, sizes, and colors for planting (1 per student)
- Empty egg cartons (enough to accommodate class size—1 indentation per student)
- Soil (enough to fill indentations in egg cartons)

Areas of Integration: Science, oral language

After reading the book, discuss what the world would be like if everyone were the exact same color, shape, size, and so on. Discuss the values of diversity and list them on the chalkboard.

Following this, show students a mixture of various seeds. Ask how the seeds are alike and how they are different.

Divide students in groups of four. Give each group of students a section of an egg carton that has four indentations in it, enough soil to fill the indentations, and one flower seed per student. Have students plant the seeds and make predictions about how the plants may vary when they are grown.

After seeds sprout and begin to grow, transplant them to a larger area. Enjoy the beauty of the various flowers.

Activity #4: Hero Collage

Materials for Activity #4:

- Poster board of various colors (1 per student)
- Old magazines and newspapers
- Photographs (brought in by students)
- Scissors
- Glue
- Markers

After reading the book, ask students to identify some modern-day heroes. Discuss that heroes can be well-known individuals or people who touch our everyday lives, like parents, teachers, coaches, and ministers.

Ask each student to choose a person whom they consider to be a hero. Have them brainstorm a list of qualities that make that person heroic. On poster board, ask students to create a collage of their heroes by bringing in photos of their hero or cutting out pictures from old magazines of the person or pictures that portray the special qualities they possess.

When the collages are complete, share them in class, and then display them within the classroom.

Related Books

Adler, D. *A Picture Book of Harriet Tubman*. New York: Scholastic, 1992.

————. *A Picture Book of Jesse Owens*. New York: Holiday House, 1992.

Adler, D. and R. Casilla. *A Picture Book of Martin Luther King, Jr.* New York: Scholastic, 1989.

Allen, Z. *Black Women Leaders of the Civil Rights Movement*. New York: Franklin Watts, 1996.

Banfield, S. *The Fifteenth Amendment: African American Men's Right to Vote*. Berkeley Heights, NJ: Enslow, 1998.

Bridges, R. *Through My Eyes*. New York: Scholastic, 1999.

Coleman, E. *White Socks Only*. Morton Grove, IL: Albert Whitman, 1996.

Gibbons, F. *Horace King: Bridges to Freedom*. Birmingham, AL: Crane Hill, 2002.

Haskins, J. *Black Eagles: African Americans in Aviation*. New York: Scholastic, 1995.

Holliday, L. *Dreaming in Color, Living in Black and White: Our Own Stories Growing Up Black in America*. New York: Pocket Books, 2000.

King, C. *Oh, Freedom! Kids Talk about the Civil Rights Movement with the People Who Made It Happen*. New York: Knopf, 1997.

Lamperti, N. *Brown Like Me*. Norwich, VT: New Victoria, 2000.

Lester, J. *Long Journey Home: Stories from Black History*. New York: Puffin, 1998.

Lowery, L. and H. Mitchell. *Martin Luther King Day*. New York: Scholastic, 1987.

Marzollo, J. and J. Pinkney. *Happy Birthday, Martin Luther King*. New York: Scholastic, 1993.

Mattern, J. *Young Martin Luther King, Jr.: I Have a Dream*. Mahwah, NJ: Troll, 1992.

McDaniel, M. *W.E.B. Dubois: Scholar and Civil Rights Activist*. New York: Franklin Watts, 1999.

McKissack, P. *Frederick Douglass: Leader against Slavery*. Berkeley Heights, NJ: Enslow, 2002.

Miller, W. *Richard Wright and the Library Card*. New York: Lee & Low, 1999.

Myers, W. *Malcolm X: A Fire Burning Brightly*. New York: HarperCollins, 2000.

Pinkney, A. *Let It Shine: Stories of Black Women Freedom Fighters*. New York: Scholastic, 2000.

Rediger, P. *Great African Americans in Civil Rights*. New York: Crabtree, 1996.

Ringgold, F. *If a Bus Could Talk: The Story of Rosa Parks*. Riverdale, NJ: Simon & Schuster, 1999.

Turck, M. *The Civil Rights Movement for Kids: A History with 21 Activities*. Chicago: Chicago Review, 2000.

Vaughan, M. *The Secret to Freedom*. New York: Lee & Low, 2001.

Related Poetry

Adoff, A. *I Am the Darker Brother: An Anthology of Modern Poems by African Americans*. New York: Pocket Books, 1997.

Anonymous. "We Shall Overcome." In *Hand in Hand: An American History through Poetry*. Ed. Lee Bennett Hopkins. Riverdale, NJ: Simon & Schuster, 1994.

Fisher, A. "Martin Luther King." In *Hand in Hand: An American History through Poetry*. Ed. Lee Bennett Hopkins. Riverdale, NJ: Simon & Schuster, 1994.

Grimes, N. *Hopscotch Love: A Family Treasury of Poems*. New York: Lothrop Lee & Shepard, 1999.

Hamilton, V. *Many Thousand Gone: African Americans from Slavery to Freedom*. New York: Knopf, 2002.

Hudson, W. ed. *Pass It On: African American Poetry for Children*. New York: Scholastic, 1993.

Hughes, L. "Dreams." In *Poetry Place Anthology*. Ed. Rosemary Alexander. New York: Scholastic, 1990.

Johnson, A. *The Other Side: Shorter Poems*. New York: Orchard, 2000.

Kennedy, X. J. "Martin Luther King Day." In *Lives: Poems about Famous Americans*. Ed. Lee Bennett Hopkins. New York: HarperCollins, 1999.

Lakritz, G. "Martin Luther King, Jr." In *Poetry Place Anthology*. Ed. Rosemary Alexander. New York: Scholastic, 1990.

Lewis, J. P. "The Many and the Few." In *Lives: Poems about Famous Americans*. Ed. Lee Bennett Hopkins. New York: HarperCollins, 1999.

Little, L. *Children of Long Ago*. New York: Lee & Low, 2000.

Moore, H. "Martin Luther King, Jr." In *A Poem a Day*. New York: Scholastic, 1997.

Myers, W. *Brown Angels: An Album of Pictures and Verse*. New York: HarperCollins, 1993.

———. *Harlem: A Poem*. New York: Scholastic, 1997.

Rochelle, B. *Words with Wings: A Treasury of African American Poetry and Art*. New York: HarperCollins, 2000.

Strickland, D., ed. *Families: Poems Celebrating the African American Experience*. Henesdale, PA: Boyds Mills Press, 1994.

Thomas, J. *The Blacker the Berry: Poems*. New York: HarperCollins, 2000.

Weatherford, C. *Remember the Bridge: Poems of a People*. New York: Philomel, 2002.

CHAPTER 6

The Civil War

Pink and Say

Patricia Polacco

(New York: Scholastic, 1994)

Book Summary: The story tells of the relationship between two fifteen-year-old Union soldiers, Pinkus Aylee (Pink) and Sheldon Russell Curtis (Say), who fought in Georgia during the Civil War. This true tale has been passed down through generations of Patricia Polacco's family.

Key Concepts: Civil War, Confederate Army, Union Army

National History Standards: 1 and 2

Activity #1: Greetings from Sheldon

> **Materials for Activity #1:**
> • Civil War slang sheets (1 per student; see handout)
> • Composition paper
> • Pencils

Areas of Integration: Reading, creative writing, oral language

After reading the book, have students discuss how the two young men must have felt about leaving their parents and homes to fight for their country. Discuss the conditions the boys lived under during this time.

Give each student a copy of the Civil War slang sheet. After discussing the terms, have students write a letter from Sheldon's perspective to his parents. The letter should include at least ten slang words used correctly.

Have students share their letters in class, then display them on a classroom bulletin board.

Civil War Slang

Chief cook and bottle washer (the boss, person capable of doing many things)

Sheet iron crackers (hardtack)

Sardine box (cap box)

Bread basket (stomach)

Greenbacks (Union paper currency)

Graybacks (Southern soldiers, lice)

Arkansas toothpick (large knife)

Pepperbox (multibarreled pistol)

Zu-Zu (Zouave soldier)

Fit to be tied (angry)

Horse sense (common sense)

Top rail #1 (the best, first class)

Hunky dory (OK or good)

Greenhorn, bugger, skunk (officers)

Snug as a bug (comfortable, cozy)

Sawbones (surgeon)

Skedaddle (run, scatter, retreat)

Hornets (bullets)

Bully (hurrah! yeah!)

Possum (a buddy)

Blowhard (braggart)

Fit as a fiddle (in good shape, healthy)

Uppity (conceited)

Scarce as hen's teeth (rare, hard to find)

Grab a root (have dinner, potato)

Tight, wallpapered (intoxicated)

Shine, bark juice, tar water (liquor)

Nokum stiff, joy juice (liquor)

Hard case (tough person)

Bluff (cheater)

Jailbird (criminal)

Hard knocks (beaten up)

Been through the mill (endured a lot)

Screamers, quick-step (diarrhea)

Played out (worn out)

Toeing the mark (obeying orders)

Jonah (someone thought to bring bad luck)

Goobers (peanuts)

Sunday soldiers, kid glove boys, parlor soldiers (insulting words for soldiers)

Fresh fish (raw recruits)

Whipped (beaten)

Source: http://www.libsci.sc.edu/miller/CivilWar.htm.

Activity #2: Sing a Song of Civil War

Materials for Activity #2:

- Words to "The Battle Cry of Freedom" songs (1 each per student; see handout)
- Words to popular Civil War songs (found at http://users.erols.com/kfraser/)
- Music to popular Civil War songs (found at http://pdmusic.org/civilwar.html)
- Chart paper
- Markers

Areas of Integration: Reading, listening, singing, analytical thinking

After reading *Pink and Say*, ask students to compare and contrast the Union's version of "The Battle Cry of Freedom" to the Confederate's version. Have them identify how the songs are similar and how they are different. List student responses on chart paper.

Following this, have students participate in singing other, more popular songs of the era, all written by Stephen C. Foster; including

- "My Old Kentucky Home"

- "Oh! Susanna"

- "Camptown Races"

- "Beautiful Dreamer"

- "Old Folks at Home"

As an extension activity, have students research the life of Stephen C. Foster to find out more about this prolific songwriter of the times.

The Battle Cry of Freedom
(Confederate version)

Music by George F. Root (1820–1895)

Our flag is proudly floating
   On the land and on the main,
Shout, shout the battle cry of Freedom!
   Beneath it oft we've conquered.
And we'll conquer oft again!
   Shout, shout the battle cry of freedom

CHORUS: Our Dixie forever!
   She's never at a loss!
Down with the eagle
   And up with the cross!
We'll rally 'round the bonny flag,
   We'll rally once again,
Shout, shout the battle cry of Freedom!

Our gallant boys have marched
   To the rolling of the drums,
Shout, shout the battle cry of Freedom!
   And the leaders in charge cry out,
"Come, boys, come!"
   Shout, shout the battle cry of Freedom

CHORUS

They have laid down their lives
   On the bloody field,
Shout, shout the battle cry of Freedom!
   Their motto is resistance—
"To tyrants we'll not yield!"
   Shout, shout the battle cry of Freedom!

CHORUS

While our boys have responded
   And to the fields have gone
Shout, shout the battle cry of Freedom!
Our noble women also
   Have aided them at home
Shout, shout the battle cry of Freedom!

CHORUS

Source: http://home.att.net/~lah-rbh/civilwar/
poem52.html

The Battle Cry of Freedom
(Union version)

By George F. Root (1820–1895)

Yes, we'll rally round the flag, boys,
   We'll rally once again
Shouting the battle cry of Freedom
   We will rally from the hillside,
We'll gather from the plain
   Shouting the battle cry of Freedom.

CHORUS: The Union forever,
   Hurrah! Boys, Hurrah!
Down with the traitors,
   Up with the stars;
While we rally round the flag, boys,
   Rally once again,
Shouting the battle cry of Freedom.

We are springing to the call
   Of our brothers gone before,
Shouting the battle cry of Freedom;
And we'll fill out vacant ranks with
   A million free men more
Shouting the battle cry of Freedom.

CHORUS

We will welcome to our numbers
   The loyal, true, and brave,
Shouting the battle cry of Freedom;
And although they may be poor,
   Not a man shall be a slave,
Shouting the battle cry of Freedom.

CHORUS

So we're springing to the call
   From the East and from the West,
Shouting the battle cry of Freedom;
And we'll hurl the rebel crew
   From the land that we love best,
Shouting the battle cry of Freedom.

CHORUS

Source: http://www.nps.gov/gett/gettkidz/gkmusic/
cwsong1.htm

Activity #3: Women of the Civil War

Materials for Activity #3:
- Civil War resource books
- Internet access
- Composition paper
- Pencils

Areas of Integration: Reading, writing, oral language

After reading the book, discuss the role of Pinkus' mother in the story. Students may be surprised to learn that some women, disguised as men, also fought in the Civil War. Have them research the lives of Sarah Emma Edmonds Seelye (also known as Franklin Thompson) and Jennie Hodgers (also known as Albert D. J. Cashier). Have them choose one of these women and write a brief biography of her life.

Black, Blue, and Gray: African Americans in the Civil War

Jim Haskins
(Riverdale, NJ: Simon & Schuster, 1998)

Book Summary: At the beginning of the Civil War, Northern armies did not want African Americans to fight with them. The Union Army, however, eventually allowed them to participate, and many historians believe that their efforts helped secure a Union victory. This book examines the Civil War and its battles and causes from the viewpoint of African Americans.

Key Concepts: Civil War, African Americans, Frederick Douglass

National History Standards: 1, 4, and 5

Activity #1: Refuting the Words of W. E. Woodward

Materials for Activity #1:
- Chart paper
- Markers
- Writing paper (1 sheet per group)

Areas of Integration: Cooperative learning, reading comprehension, oral expression

After reading and discussing *Black, Blue, and Gray: African Americans in the Civil War*, have students read the quote from W. E. Woodward given on p. 3:

The American Negroes are the only people in the history of the world, so far as I know, that ever became free without any effort of their own. The Civil War was not their business. They had not started the war nor ended it. They twanged banjos around the railroad stations, sang melodious spirituals, and believed that some Yankees would soon come along and give each of them forty acres of land and a mule.

Ask students the following questions:

1. Do you believe this statement to be historically accurate? Why or why not?

2. If not, why do you believe W. E. Woodward made such a statement?

3. How is prejudice evident in the statement?

Divide students into seven small groups. Assign each group a chapter and ask students to record facts from their chapter that refute Woodward's statement. Any facts that document the efforts of African Americans during the Civil War would be appropriate. Each group can transfer its list of facts to chart paper. Hang the lists around the room in the order of the chapters in the book. Allow the groups an opportunity to present their facts and accept questions from the other members of the class.

Activity #2: Analyzing Recruitment Posters, Newspaper Ads, and Editorials

> **Materials for Activity #2:**
>
> - Poster paper
> - Markers, crayons, and paints
> - Writing paper
> - Word processor

Areas of Integration: Critical thinking, creative writing, artistic expression

After reading and discussing the book and Frederick Douglass' role in the recruitment of African Americans, have students analyze the recruitment poster on page 49, the newspaper ad on page 64, and the editorial on page 65. Ask students the following questions:

1. Were there risks involved for the African Americans who enlisted in the Union Army? If so, what were they?

2. Was there unequal treatment for the African Americans who served?

3. Were the recruitment poster and editorial misleading to those who read them? Why?

4. Why would Frederick Douglass, who was an African American, mislead men who were considering joining the Union Army?

Have students consider this discussion and then design a recruitment poster or write an editorial that would be a more honest representation of the risks involved for African Americans in the Civil War. Encourage creativity as well as historical accuracy.

Activity #3: Story Pyramids

Materials for Activity #3:

• Story pyramids (1 per student; below)

Areas of Integration: Critical thinking, creative writing

Story Pyramid

1. _____

2. _____ _____

3. _____ _____ _____

4. _____ _____ _____ _____

5. _____ _____ _____ _____ _____

6. _____ _____ _____ _____ _____ _____

7. _____ _____ _____ _____ _____ _____ _____

8. _____ _____ _____ _____ _____ _____ _____ _____

Student _____

Name of Book _____

Author _____

Source: http://www.canteach.ca/elementary/novel10.html

After reading and discussing *Black, Blue, and Gray: African Americans in the Civil War*, ask students to make a story pyramid on one character from the book who interests them. After choosing a character, students can utilize the following pattern:

1. Name of character

2. Two words describing the character

3. Three words describing the setting where the character's actions take place

4. Four words stating a problem faced by the character

5. Five words describing one event in which the character was involved

6. Six words describing a second event in which the character was involved

7. Seven words describing a third event in which the character was involved

8. Eight words describing the resolution to the character's problem or the outcome of his or her involvement in the Civil War

Harriet Beecher Stowe: Author of Uncle Tom's Cabin

LeeAnne Gelletly
(Broomall, PA: Chelsea House Publishers, 2001)

Book Summary: Harriet Beecher Stowe was an unusual woman for her time. An abolitionist, she was not afraid to speak out against slavery. She wrote her controversial novel *Uncle Tom's Cabin* in 1852, which eventually was translated into twenty-three languages. Stone traveled to Washington, D.C., to speak with President Abraham Lincoln to encourage him to sign the Emancipation Proclamation.

Key Concepts: Slavery, emancipation, Civil War

National History Standards: 1 and 4

Activity #1: Think, Pair, Share

Materials for Activity #1:
• Think, pair, share questions given in the following list

Areas of Integration: Critical thinking, cooperative learning, expressive language

After reading and discussing *Harriet Beecher Stowe*, choose a think, pair, share question from the following list:

1. What do you think it would be like to live during the time of slavery?

2. Pretend you were an abolitionist. What do you think you might have done to help end slavery?

3. Pretend you are an abolitionist. What might you say to others to convince them that slavery is wrong?

4. Do you think it would have been more difficult for a man or a woman to be actively involved as an abolitionist during the time of slavery? Why?

5. Do you think that President Lincoln would have approved of the Fugitive Slave Act of 1850? Why or why not?

6. What impact did *Uncle Tom's Cabin* have on the people in the North? In the South?

7. What characters in this book, other than Harriet Beecher Stowe, helped end slavery? What did they do to make a difference?

Ask students to follow these procedures. First, give students one or two minutes of think time (depending on the complexity of the question) to consider an answer to the question. They may want to jot down their ideas. Second, ask students to find a partner. Allow three to five minutes for each pair to share, compare, and justify their answers and to debate any differences they might have. Third, ask for volunteers to share their answers with the large group.

Source: Rasinski, T. & Padak, N. (1996). *Holistic reading strategies: Teaching children who find reading difficult.* Englewood Cliffs, NJ: Merrill/Prentice Hall.

Activity #2: Prediction Charts

> **Materials for Activity #2:**
> - Prediction charts (1 per student; see handout)
> - Large chart paper

Areas of Integration: Predicting, listening skills, auditory memory

Before reading the book *Harriet Beecher Stowe,* give each student a prediction chart. Discuss the title and front cover of the book. Turn to chapter 1 and present the title, "A New England Beginning." Ask students to write on their charts what they believe chapter 1 will be about. Volunteers may want to share their predictions. Then read chapter 1. As you read, make a word wall of the vocabulary words in bold type (to be used in Activity #3) on chart paper. Now ask students to write what actually happened in the chapter. Ask students to compare their predictions with what actually happened. Continue these procedures for chapters 2 through 6. Allow students to share how accurate their predictions were and how the title of each chapter helped them make good predictions.

Prediction Chart

	What I Predict Will Happen	What Actually Happened
Chapter 1		
Chapter 2		
Chapter 3		
Chapter 4		
Chapter 5		
Chapter 6		

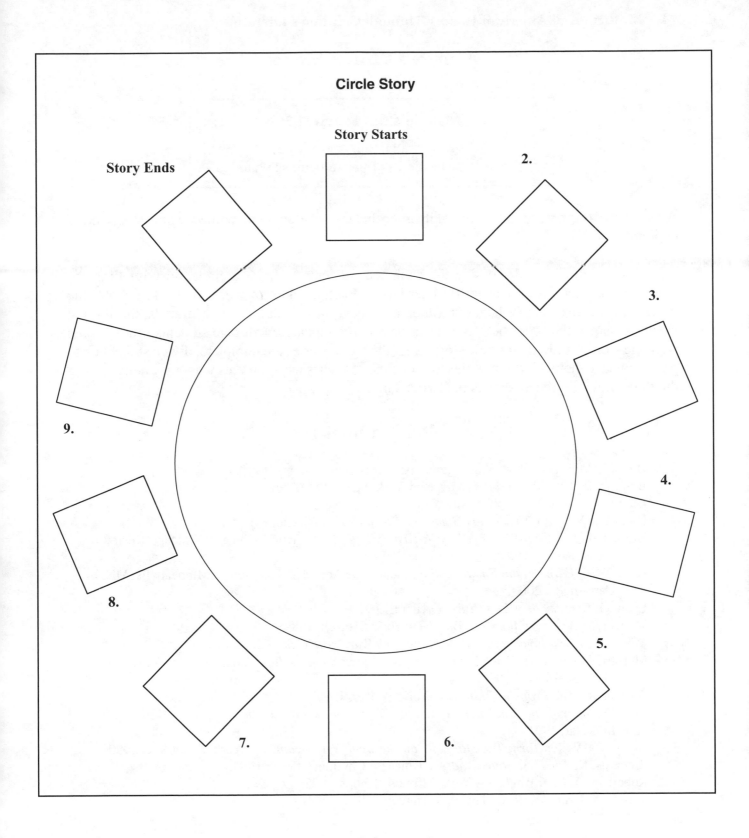

Circle Story

Story Starts

Story Ends

2.

3.

4.

5.

6.

7.

8.

9.

Activity #3: Circle Stories

> ### Materials for Activity #3:
> • Word wall (from Activity #2)
> • Circle story handouts (1 per student; see handout)

Areas of Integration: Listening skills, vocabulary development, written expression, verbal expression

After reading and discussing the book, ask students to write a circle story retelling the main events in the life of Harriet Beecher Stowe. Each main event will be placed in one of the blocks on the circle story handout. Students may want to make a rough draft listing the ten events in sequential order before placing them in the blocks. Encourage students to use words from the word wall in their circle story. After the circle stories are complete, divide students into pairs and have them tell their stories to each other. Discuss with students what they believe to be the three most significant events in Harriet's life.

Related Books

Biros, F. *Dog Jack*. New Wilmington, PA: Sonrise Publications, 1990.
Bunting, E. *The Blue and the Gray*. New York: Scholastic, 1996.
Hakim, J. *War, Terrible, War*. New York: Oxford University Press, 1994.
Hamilton, V. *Many Thousands Gone*. New York: Alfred A. Knopf, 1993.
Herbert, J. *The Civil War for Kids: A History with 21 Activities*. Chicago: Chicago Review Press, 1999.
King, W. *Children of the Emancipation*. Picture the American Past Series. Minneapolis, MN: Carolrhoda, 2000.
Lyon, G. *Cecil's Story*. New York: Orchard, 1991.
Meltzer, M. *Voices of the Civil War*. New York: Crowell, 1989.
Moore, K. *If You Lived at the Time of the Civil War*. New York: Scholastic, 1994.
Murphy, J. *The Boys' War: Confederate and Union Soldiers Talk about the Civil War*. New York: Scholastic, 1990.
Ransom, C. *The Promise Quilt*. New York: Walker, 1999.
Ray, D. *Behind the Blue and the Gray: The Soldier's Life in the Civil War*. New York: Lodestar, 1991.
———. *A Nation Torn: The Story of How the Civil War Began*. New York: Scholastic, 1990.
Richards, K. *The Gettysburg Address*. Chicago: Children's Press, 1992.
Robertson, J. *Civil War!* New York: Alfred A. Knopf, 1992.
Turner, A. *Drummer Boy*. New York: HarperCollins, 1998.

Related Poetry

Kennedy, X. J. "The Loneliness of Lincoln." In *Hand in Hand: An American History through Poetry*. Ed. Lee Bennett Hopkins. Riverdale, NJ: Simon & Schuster, 1994.

CHAPTER 7
Immigration

Bound for America: The Forced Migration of Africans to the New World

Jim Haskins and K. Benson
(New York: Lothrop Lee and Shepard, 1999)

Book Summary: This book details the history of slavery in Europe and Africa and the flourish and decline of the New World slave trade market. Between 1500 and 1850, millions of Africans were captured and savagely shipped across the Atlantic Ocean to a life of inhumane servitude. The author describes in painful detail the capture and treatment of the slaves before and during the Middle Passage, the slave mutinies, and the eventual end of slavery.

Key Concepts: Slavery, slave trade market, Middle Passage, mutiny, coffles, slave ship, slave holding pens, branding, leg and neck irons, guineamen or slavers, porridge, "dancing the slaves," Amistad Revolt

National History Standards: 4, 5, and 7

Activity #1: *Bound for America* Crossword Puzzle

Materials for Activity #1:

- Graph paper with ½″ squares (2 per student)
- *Bound for America* vocabulary sheet (see handout)
- Composition paper

Areas of Integration: Vocabulary development, writing

After reading *Bound for America*, divide students into pairs and ask them to define the terms from the story on the vocabulary sheet provided. When the pairs are finished, go over the definitions together as a class.

Tell students that they will each be creating a crossword puzzle for a classmate using terms and definitions from the story. Provide each student with two pieces of squared graph paper from which they will create the crossword puzzle and an answer key. Explain that each puzzle must use at least fifteen of the twenty terms provided. Students will write their puzzle clues in "down" and "across" format on composition paper. Students will create an answer key for the puzzle on the second piece of graph paper. After all puzzles have been constructed, students can exchange them in class and complete each other's puzzle.

Activity #2: Create an Artifact

Materials for Activity #2:

- Resource books on slavery or Internet access
- 6″ × 8″ index cards (1 per student)
- Assorted materials from which students can create artifacts, such as:

markers	toothpicks	colored
string	tissue paper	masking tape
poster paints	scissors	cardboard
aluminum foil	paper towel	paperclips
scraps of fabric	rolls	yarn
pipe cleaners	dowel rods	glue

Areas of Integration: Creative expression, critical thinking, research skills, writing, problem solving

While reading *Bound for America*, draw students' attention to the illustrations included throughout the book. Discuss the brutal use of the leg, neck, and branding irons depicted on pages 20–21, 25, and 26–27. Examine the sculptures shown on page 11. Focus students' attention on the speculum oris given on page 33 and the cat-o'-nine-tails pictured on page 34.

After discussing the inhumane treatment of slaves throughout history, tell students that they will be choosing and creating an artifact from the slavery era. Before they begin, they must research the artifact using resource books or the Internet. They will then use a variety of materials to create a replica of the artifact. Students will write a description of the artifact on the index card and tell how it relates to the slave era.

When students are finished creating their artifacts, have them share them in class. Assemble the artifacts and description cards and display them in a display case within the school for others to view and learn about the inhumane treatment of slaves throughout history.

Bound for America

Vocabulary Sheet

1. Slavery _____

2. Imprison _____

3. Africa _____

4. Mali _____

5. Slave traders _____

6. Neck iron _____

7. Branding iron _____

8. Cat-o'-nine-tails _____

9. Holding pens _____

10. Sharks _____

11. Coffles _____

12. Trunks _____

13. Barracoons _____

14. Branding _____

15. Leg irons _____

16. Guineamen _____

17. Sea biscuit _____

18. Amistad _____

19. Mutiny _____

20. Inquisition _____

Activity #3: A Picture's Worth a Thousand Words

Materials for Activity #3:

- Chart paper
- Marker
- Cover illustration of *Bound for America*

Areas of Integration: Analytical thinking, writing, self-expression

Have students examine the illustration on the front cover of the book. Ask them: How do you think the man feels? How would you feel in similar circumstances? Why might he have his eyes closed? Why do you think his head is bowed?

After examining and discussing the illustration, have students brainstorm together a list of possible titles or captions for the illustration by Floyd Cooper. Upon completion of the brainstorming activity, have students vote for the title or caption that they feel best captures the mood and theme of the illustration.

As a follow-up activity, students can research biographic information on the artist, Floyd Cooper, and share their findings in class.

Coming to America: The Story of Immigration

Betsy Maestro
(New York: Scholastic, 1996)

Book Summary: This informational book describes immigration to America from the great Ice Age to the present time. It discusses why people have come to America, the journeys they made to this country, and the areas in the United States in which each group settled. During each period of history, this book documents which immigrants arrived and what their lives were like in their new homes.

Key Concepts: Immigration, Ellis Island

National History Standards: 5, 6, and 7

Activity #1: Immigration Time Line

Materials for Activity #1:

• Immigration time lines (1 per student; see below)
• World map

Areas of Integration: Auditory memory, critical thinking, oral language

As you are reading *Coming to America: The Story of Immigration*, have students complete the immigration time line by writing in which ethnic groups or nationalities have immigrated to America. Attach a large world map to a bulletin board. Allow students to take turns drawing arrows from each of the countries on the time line to the United States. On the arrow ask students to write the dates during which the immigrants came to America. Discuss with students the reasons why immigrants move to the United States.

Immigration Time Line

Ice Age _____

1492 _____

1500s and 1600s _____

1619 to 1800s _____

By 1700 _____

1700s _____

1800s _____

End of 1800s _____

January 1, 1892 _____

After the 1940s _____

After the 1950s _____

Today _____

Answers to Immigration Time Line

Ice Age: Nomads from Asia

1492: Christopher Columbus

1500s and 1600s: Immigrants from Europe

1619 to 1800s: Slaves from Africa

By 1700: Immigrants from Netherlands, Sweden, Germany, Finland, and Wales

1700s: Settlers from Scotland, Ireland, and Switzerland

1800s: Immigrants from Norway, China, and Mexico moved west

End of 1800s: Immigrants from Italy, Poland, Turkey, Greece, Hungary, and Serbia

January 1, 1892: Ellis Island opens

After the 1940s: Refugees from Europe

After the 1950s: Immigrants from Southeast Asia, Cuba, and Haiti

Today: Immigrants from Russia, Europe, Asia, Mexico, South and Central America, the Middle East, the West Indies, and Africa

Activity #2: Valuing Diversity

Materials for Activity #2:
- Chart paper

Areas of Integration: Oral language, critical thinking

After reading and discussing the book, ask students to brainstorm the ways in which our nation benefits from the diversity we experience as a result of immigration. Have them brainstorm the advantages of diversity in the areas of art, music, literature, theater, or foods. Ask each student to bring in one example of art, music, literature, theater, or food to share with classmates.

Activity #3: Interviewing an Immigrant

Materials for Activity #3:
- Guest speaker
- Writing paper

Areas of Integration: Oral language, critical thinking

After reading and discussing *Coming to America: The Story of Immigration,* invite an immigrant to speak to the class about his or her immigration experience. Prepare students in advance by telling them the country from which this person immigrated. Ask students to write down the questions that they would like to ask this person during the visit. Allow the guest speaker to begin by telling his or her immigration story; follow with students' questions. Consider having a panel of guest speakers, so that students can compare different immigration experiences.

Journey to Ellis Island

Carol Bierman
(New York: Hyperion, 1998)

Book Summary: *Journey to Ellis Island* is the story of Yehuda and his family and their emigration from Russia to America. When they arrived, Yehuda had to prove to officials that he was healthy because he had lost part of the ring finger on his right hand. The family settled in New York City, and his English name became Julius Weinstein.

Key Concepts: Immigration, Ellis Island

National History Standard: 5

Activity #1: My Family's Immigration to America

> **Materials for Activity #1:**
> - World map
> - Yarn
> - Pushpins

Areas of Integration: Oral language, map skills

After reading and discussing *Journey to Ellis Island,* help students find Russia on the map and discuss the distance traveled by Yehuda's family to get to America. Stretch a piece of yarn from Russia to New York City and attach with pushpins. Ask students to go home and interview their parents, grandparents, or aunts and uncles to determine the countries from which their ancestors came. Allow each student to attach pieces of yarn from those countries to the region in America where their ancestors settled. Have students discuss why their ancestors might have left their homelands and ask them to determine whether there is a pattern to the countries from which the people emigrated.

Activity #2: Park in a Pack Activities on Ellis Island

Materials for Activity #2:

• Park in a Pack from the National Park Service

Areas of Integration: Problem solving, critical thinking, oral language

After reading the book and discussing the history of Ellis Island, contact the education specialist at the National Park Service at 212-363-3200 or by e-mail at stli_info@nps.gov. Ask for the Park in a Pack kit for Ellis Island. This curriculum-based traveling educational kit is free for two-week loan periods to educators who teach grades 4–8. It includes a teaching guide, three videos, and educational activities. The activities allow students to investigate the medical exams, legal inspections, citizenship tests, and mental tests that immigrants had to undergo before they could enter the country and become citizens. For more information, access the National Park Service website at http://www.nps.gov/stli/serv02.htm and the Park in a Pack website at http://www.nps/gov/stli/page1.htm.

Activity #3: Comparing and Contrasting *Journey to Ellis Island* with *When Jessie Came across the Sea*

Materials for Activity #3:

• *When Jessie Came across the Sea* by A. Hest (Candlewick Press, 1997)

Areas of Integration: Critical thinking, cooperative learning, creative writing

After reading and discussing both books, divide students into small groups. Ask students to compare Yehuda's journey to America with Jessie's journey. Draw a large Venn diagram on the chalkboard or on an overhead transparency. Label one of the circles "Yehuda's Journey"; and label the other circle "Jessie's Journey." Have students consider the following:

• The reasons why the characters left their homelands

• Their method of transportation

• Their experiences during the trip

• The emotions they experienced

• Their experiences at Ellis Island

- The location in which they settled

- Their lives in America

Next, have the students in each small group create a short skit describing a meeting between Yehuda and Jessie. Have students include how and when they met and what happened as a result of their meeting. Allow students to present their skits to the class.

Related Books

Atkin, S. *Voices from the Fields*. New York: Scholastic, 1993.
Bunting, E. *Dreaming of America: An Ellis Island Story*. Mahwah, NJ: Troll, 2000.
———. *How Many Days to America?* New York: Trumpet, 1988.
———. *A Picnic in October*. New York: Harcourt, 1999.
Czech, J. *An American Face*. Washington, DC: Child Welfare League of America, 2000.
Durbin, W. *The Journal of Otto Peltonen a Finnish Immigrant*. New York: Scholastic, 2000.
Fahey, K. *The Japanese*. We Came to North America. New York: Crabtree, 2001.
Freedman, R. *Immigrant Kids*. New York: Scholastic, 1980.
Hesse, K. *Letters from Rifka*. New York: Scholastic, 1992.
Hest, A. *When Jessie Came across the Sea*. Cambridge, MA: Candlewick Press, 1997.
Isaacs, S. *Life at Ellis Island*. Chicago: Heinemann Library, 2002.
Jimenez, F. *La Mariposa*. Boston: Houghton Mifflin, 2000.
Levine, E., and W. Paramenter. *If Your Name Was Changed at Ellis Island*. New York: Scholastic, 1993.
Mikaelsen, B. *Red Midnight*. New York: HarperCollins, 2002.
Moss, M. *Hannah's Journal: The Story of an Immigrant Girl*. San Diego, CA: Silver Whistle, 2000.
Nye, N. *Habibi*. New York: Pocket Books, 1999.
Oberman, S. *The Always Prayer Shawl*. New York: Puffin, 1997.
Partridge, E. *Oranges on Golden Mountain*. New York: Dutton, 2001.
Pastore, C. *Aniela Kaminski's Story: A Voyage from Poland During World War II*. New York: Berkley Publishing, 2001.
———. *Fiona McGilray's Story: A Voyage from Ireland in 1849*. New York: Berkley Publishing, 2001.
Polacco, P. *The Keeping Quilt*. Riverdale, NJ: Simon & Schuster, 1998.
Schanzer, R. *Escape to America: A True Story*. New York: HarperCollins, 2000.
Springstubb, T. *The Vietnamese Americans*. Immigrants in America. San Diego, CA: Lucent Books, 2001.
Tarbescu, E. *Annushka's Voyage*. New York: Clarion, 1998.
Todd, A. *Italian Immigrants, 1880–1920*. Mankato, MN: Blue Earth Books, 2002.
Weiss, E. *Ellis Island Days*. New York: Aladdin, 2002.
Whitman, S. *Immigrant Children*. Minneapolis, MN: Carolrhoda Books, 2000.
Woodruff, E. *The Memory Coat*. New York: Scholastic, 1999.
———. *The Orphan of Ellis Island: Time-Travel Adventure*. New York: Scholastic, 1997.
Yep, L. *The Journal of Wong Ming-Chung: A Chinese Miner, California, 1852*. New York: Scholastic, 2000.

Yin. *Coolies.* New York: Philomel, 2001.
Ziefert, H. *When I First Came to This Land.* New York: Putnam, 1998.

Related Poetry

Field, E. "Both My Grandmothers." In *Celebrating America: A Collection of Poems and Images of the American Spirit.* Ed. Laura Whipple. New York: Philomel, 1994.
Mak, K. *My Chinatown: One Year in Poems.* New York: HarperCollins, 2001.

CHAPTER *8*

World War II and the Holocaust

So Far from the Sea

Eve Bunting
(New York: Scholastic, 1998)

Book Summary: The story, set in 1972, describes memories of thirty years ago. A seven-year-old Japanese American girl, named Laura, journeys with her family to view the grave site of her grandfather at a World War II campsite at the Manzanar War Relocation Center. Here her father, as a child, and grandfather were detained years earlier. Laura's father struggles to explain the unfair treatment of 10,000 Japanese ancestors after the bombing of Pearl Harbor and the need to accept past things "that cannot be changed."

Key Concepts: Pearl Harbor, World War II, prison camp, Manzanar

National History Standards: 1, 3, 4, and 7

Activity #1: Open-minded Portrait

> **Materials for Activity #1:**
> - Black construction paper (1 per student)
> - White construction paper (1 per student)
> - Scissors (1 pair per student)
> - Crayons, markers, colored pencils
> - Stapler and staples

Areas of Integration: Creative expression, writing, oral language

After reading and discussing Eve Bunting's *So Far from the Sea*, have students reflect on the character of Laura Iwasaki. Ask them: What do you know about her? How do you learn about Laura? What do her words tell you about the kind of child that she is? What do Laura's actions say about her?

Give each student a sheet of black construction paper and a sheet of white construction paper. Ask them to draw a silhouette of Laura's head and shoulders on the black paper. Once the silhouette is complete, have students place the black piece of construction paper on top of the white and cut both pieces out into the silhouette of the main character. Staple the black sheet on top of the white piece of paper.

On the white paper, ask students to write about and draw Laura's thoughts throughout the book. They may write sentences, phrases, or words or draw pictures of things that Laura encountered on her visit to the Manzanar War Relocation Center.

When students have finished, ask them to share their character portraits with the class. Use the portraits to create a classroom bulletin board with an appropriate title chosen by the class.

Source: Tompkins, G. E. (1997). *Literacy for the twenty-first century: A balanced approach.* Upper Saddle River: NJ: Merrill/Prentice Hall.

Activity #2: Focused Free Write: What Does It Mean to Be an American?

> **Materials for Activity #2:**
> - Student journals or composition paper
> - Pencils
> - Chart paper
> - Markers

Areas of Integration: Writing, critical thinking, oral language

Before reading *So Far from the Sea*, ask students to take out their journals or give them each a sheet of composition paper. Tell them that today they are going to be reading a story about Japanese Americans who were imprisoned during World War II in a camp in eastern California at the Manzanar War Relocation Center after the Japanese bombed Pearl Harbor.

Explain to students that focused free writing is a technique often used by writers to activate their thoughts on a certain topic. The rules for focused free writing are as follows:

1. The writer must write on the assigned topic.

2. The writer must write nonstop for a two-minute time period on the assigned topic.

3. The writer may write words, phrases, and/or sentences that relate to the topic.

4. After two minutes, when time is called, the writer stops writing.

On the chalkboard, write the following writing prompt: What does it mean to be an American? Have students engage in the focused free-writing activity. When they are done, ask for student volunteers to share their thoughts. Record their thoughts on chart paper.

After reading the story, return to the writing prompt and discuss students' thoughts and feelings.

Activity #3: Pearl Harbor: Group Presentations

Materials for Activity #3:

• Internet access

Areas of Integration: Creative and critical thinking, creative expression, writing, oral language

After reading *So Far from the Sea*, have students access the following Internet website on Pearl Harbor: http://www.surfnetkids.com/pearlharbor.htm. Divide students into five groups. Assign each group to explore a section of the information provided at this website. Assign the information as follows:

Group #1—Attack at Pearl Harbor

Group #2—December 7: Today in History

Group #3—Pearl Harbor Remembered

Group #4—Radio in 1941

Group #5—U.S.S. *Arizona* Memorial at Pearl Harbor

Each group will use the information provided at the website to create an informative, original, and creative presentation that will be presented to the class. Students may decide within their groups how best to present the information in an original, creative way. Ideas for presentation might include recreating President Franklin D. Roosevelt's radio speech, drawing propaganda posters, or writing a newspaper article about the bombing of Pearl Harbor. If the presentations can be videotaped, the groups could review their presentations and reflect upon the quality of their group project.

After students have finished their research and created their presentations, they may perform them before the class. Following the presentations, ask students to review what they learned from the presentations made about Pearl Harbor.

Faithful Elephants: A True Story of Animals, People, and War

Yukio Tsuchiya
(Boston: Houghton Mifflin, 1988)

Book Summary: During World War II, bombs fell frequently on Tokyo. Officials at the Ueno Zoo were afraid that if a bomb hit the zoo the animals might escape and run wild in the city. For this reason, the army commanded that all animals be killed. This is the story of three elephants and their last days.

Key Concepts: World War II, impact of war

National History Standards: 4 and 7

Activity #1: Book Critique

> **Materials for Activity #1:**
> • Book selection committee forms (1 per student; see below)

Areas of Integration: Critical thinking, writing

After reading and discussing *Faithful Elephants: A True Story of Animals, People, and War,* ask students to become a part of a book selection committee. Have students critique *Faithful Elephants* by documenting the strengths and weaknesses of the book and discussing whether they would recommend this book to another class studying World War II. Ask each student to fill out a book selection committee form. If the majority of students recommend this book, it can become part of a class book, "The Best Books We've Read." Throughout the year, students can add additional books related to units of study.

Book Selection Committee Form

Author: _____

Title: _____

Illustrator: _____

City Where Published and Publisher: _____

_____

Publication Date: _____

Strengths of this Book: _____

_____

_____

_____

Weaknesses of this book: _____

_____

_____

_____

Recommendations: _____

_____

_____

_____

Activity #2: Rewriting *Faithful Elephants* from the Elephants' Point of View

> **Materials for Activity #2:**
>
> • Writing paper

Areas of Integration: Creative writing, oral language

After reading the book, ask students how they think the elephants felt as they were becoming weak from lack of food and water. Ask students to rewrite those portions of the story describing the deaths of John, Tonky, or Wanly, from the elephant's point of view. Encourage students to provide vivid descriptions of what the elephants were thinking, feeling, and doing during this tragic time. Allow students to share their stories in small groups.

Activity #3: Alternatives to Killing the Elephants

> **Materials for Activity #3:**
>
> • Story webs (1 per student)
> • Chart paper

Areas of Integration: Problem solving

After reading and discussing *Faithful Elephants: A True Story of Animals, People, and War*, have students complete a story web to document the story's setting, main characters, title and author, problem, and solution (see handout). Then ask students to consider whether they believe that the army's solution to this problem was the best or the only solution. Have students brainstorm other solutions to this problem and document them on chart paper. Discuss the feasibility of each solution and possible reasons why these alternative solutions were not considered by the army.

A Picture Book of Anne Frank

David Adler
(New York: Scholastic, 1993)

Book Summary: *A Picture Book of Anne Frank* recounts the courageous life of a young Jewish girl during the Holocaust.

Story Web

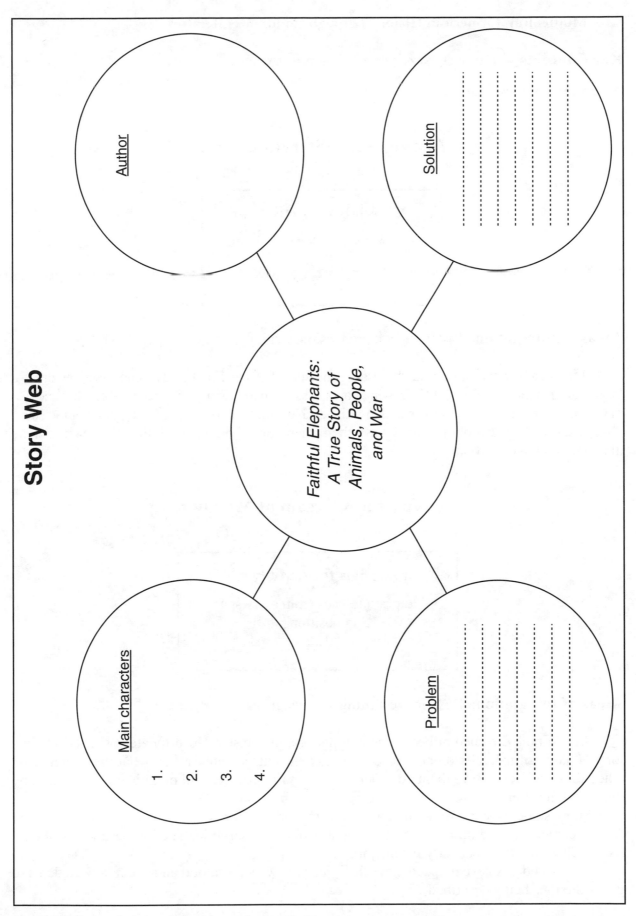

Author

Solution

Faithful Elephants: A True Story of Animals, People, and War

Main characters

1.

2.

3.

4.

Problem

Key Concepts: Holocaust, Nazi, persecution, prison camps

National History Standards: 1 and 5

Activity #1: A Star for Courage

> **Materials for Activity #1:**
> - 8½″ × 11″ drawing paper
> - Pencils
> - Scissors

Areas of Integration: Listening comprehension, writing

After reading the story and discussing the life of Anne Frank, have each student draw a large star on a piece of 8½″ × 11″ drawing paper. Ask them to identify five ways in which Anne displayed courage throughout her life and to write each example on one of the five points of the star.

After students cut out the stars, have them share their thoughts with the class. Stars can be displayed in the classroom.

Activity #2: A Dream of My Own

> **Materials for Activity #2:**
> - Help wanted ads from a newspaper
> - Composition paper
> - Pencils

Areas of Integration: Descriptive writing, oral language

Anne Frank dreamed of becoming a writer or a movie star. Unfortunately, she did not live long enough to make her dream come true. Ask students to think about what they want to be when they are older. Have them consider the necessary qualities and qualifications required by that particular job.

Show students some want ads for jobs from a newspaper and ask them to write a want ad for the career they are thinking about without naming the job title. The job description should list specific qualities necessary for the job.

When students have finished, have them read the want ads aloud and ask fellow students to guess the jobs being described.

Activity #3: Eating Your Way to Good Health

> **Materials for Activity #3:**
> - Anne Frank quotation written on chalkboard (below)
> - My Daily Diet sheet (1 per student; see handout)
> - Chart paper
> - Colored markers
> - Encyclopedia or health references
> - Composition paper

In the twenty one months that we've spent here, we have been through a good many "food cycles" . . . periods in which one has nothing else to eat but one particular dish or kind of vegetable. We had nothing but endive for a long time, day in, day out, endive with sand, endive without sand, stew with endive, boiled or "en cassarole," then it was spinach, and after that followed by kohlrabi, salsify, cucumbers, tomatoes, sauerkraut, etc., each according to the season. (Anne Frank—April 13, 1944)

Areas of Integration: Nutrition, health, science, reading, writing, oral language

Anne Frank and her sister, Margot, died of hunger and disease in a German concentration camp not long after Anne wrote the above entry into her diary.

Read and discuss the quotation above and the importance of a varied, well-balanced diet to good nutrition. Have students brainstorm a list of nutrition-related diseases. Write these on chart paper. Add to the list the following: anemia, anorexia, bulimia, osteoporosis, rickets, scurvy, beriberi, pellagra, and goiter.

Over the next three days, ask students to record what they eat during a day and identify the food group from which the foods originate. When complete, have students discuss their diets in small groups with each other. Ask them: Are your diets more varied than Anne Frank's diet? Do you consider your diet to be well-balanced?

Refer back to the list of nutrition-related diseases. Divide students into pairs to research one of the diseases. Ask them to find out the following:

1. What causes the condition?

2. What are the symptoms?

3. Where is the disease found in the world today?

4. What treatments are available?

5. Do you think the disease will ever be eliminated? Why or why not?

Have pairs report their findings to the whole group.

My Daily Diet

Day #1

Breakfast   Lunch   Dinner

Day #2

Breakfast   Lunch   Dinner

Day #3

Breakfast   Lunch   Dinner

Related Books

Colman, P. *Rosie the Riveter: Women Working on the Home Front in World War II.* New York: Crown Publishers, 1995.

Granfield, L. *High-Flight: A Story of World War II.* Plattsburgh, NY: Tundra Books, 1999.

Hurwitz, J. *Anne Frank: Life in Hiding.* New York: Avon Books, 1988.

Innocenti, R. *Rose Blanche.* San Diego, CA: Harcourt Brace, 1985.

Lakin, P. *Don't Forget.* New York: Tambourine Books, 1994.

Polacco, P. *The Butterfly.* New York: Scholastic, 2000.

Uchida, Y. *The Bracelet.* New York: Philomel, 1993.

Related Poetry and Songs

Brand, Oscar. "Gee, Mom, I Want to Go Home." In *From Sea to Shining Sea: A Treasury of American Folklore and Folk Songs.* Ed. Amy Cohen. New York: Scholastic, 1993.

Glaser, Isabel Joshlin. "The Last Good War—and Afterward." In *Hand in Hand: An American History through Poetry.* Ed. Lee Bennett Hopkins. Riverdale, NJ: Simon & Schuster, 1994.

Sandburg, Carl. "The People, Yes." In *Hand in Hand: An American History through Poetry.* Ed. Lee Bennett Hopkins. Riverdale, NJ: Simon & Schuster, 1994.

CHAPTER 9

Vietnam

The Wall

Eve Bunting
(New York: Clarion, 1990)

Book Summary: This book tells the story of a father and son who visit the Vietnam Veterans Memorial in Washington, D.C., to locate the name of the grandfather the youngster never knew. The story, told from the child's point of view, brings out the sorrow of the war sacrifices made by American military veterans serving their country and the impact of the war on their families and loved ones. The significance of the wall is explained, and the different expressions of tribute left by family members at the memorial are explored.

Key Concepts: Vietnam War, veteran, memorial, Vietnam Veterans Memorial, "missing in action"

National History Standards: 3 and 4

Activity #1: Remembering Vietnam Veterans

Materials for Activity #1:
- Composition paper
- Pencils

Areas of Integration: Writing, creative expression

After reading *The Wall*, have students identify the items mentioned or illustrated in the book that people left at the wall (flowers, flags, an old teddy bear, photographs, and letters) as remembrances of those individuals who gave their lives in the Vietnam War. Discuss the significance of each item and ask students to talk about the people who may have left each item at the wall.

Following the discussion, ask students either to write letters to actual Vietnam veterans or to compose remembrance letters or poems for those veterans whose names are listed on the Vietnam Veterans Memorial in Washington, D.C. A local Veteran's Administration office could assist in securing the names and addresses of living veterans.

When students are finished with their compositions, mail the letters and poems to their destinations. Information about the Vietnam Veterans Memorial can be obtained from

900 Ohio Drive, SW
Washington, DC 20242, USA
Phone: (202) 426-6841
E-mail: National_Mall@nps.gov

Activity #2: Class Buddy Wall

Materials for Activity #2:

- Plaster of Paris mix
- Water
- Empty quart milk cartons
- Tracing paper
- Crayons (with paper coverings removed)

Areas of Integration: Creative expression, writing, oral language

In the story, the father makes a rubbing of his father's name from the wall in order to remember him and his place in history. As a class, have the students make a "brick" or something similar from plaster of Paris. Students can use empty quart milk containers, with one long panel removed, as molds for the bricks. When bricks are partially dried, ask each student to trace his or her name in the brick.

When bricks are completely dry, build a "wall" of classroom buddies. Have students use tracing paper and old crayons, whose paper has been removed, to rub over the names of their classmates.

Following this, place slips of paper with classmates' names written on them in a box. Have each student randomly pull the name of a classmate from the box, making sure that students do not draw their own names. Students will then write a paragraph about the classmate in which they recall specific, positive interactions with the classmate. They might write about a project that they worked on together or some event they attended together.

When complete, the students can orally share their memories and have classmates guess about whom they have written. The paragraphs can be displayed, along with the rubbing of the students' names, on a wall of the classroom.

Activity #3: A Memorial for Someone Special

> **Materials for Activity #3:**
> • Construction paper (1 per student)
> • Crayons, markers, colored pencils
> • Modeling clay (a cupful for each student)
> • Index cards (1 per student)

Areas of Integration: Creative expression, oral language, writing

After reading *The Wall*, ask students to describe any other monuments they might have visited in Washington, D.C., such as the Lincoln Memorial, the Washington Monument, and the Jefferson Memorial. Students can learn more about monuments and memorials in Washington, D.C. by visiting the following website: http://www.washington-landmarks.com/landmarks.html.

Following this, ask students to think about a person who has meant a lot to them who is no longer living. The person could be a relative, an acquaintance, or someone from history. Ask them to think about the qualities possessed by that person that made him or her a special person and one who should be remembered in a special way.

Next, ask students to design a monument or memorial in honor of that person. Students should begin by drafting on paper a prototype for the monument. After designs have been created, students can use modeling clay to create a small replica of the monument. Encourage each student to inscribe a word on his or her monument that summarizes the best quality of the person for whom the monument was created.

After monuments have dried, students can share them in class, telling whom the monument memorializes and why that particular person was chosen. Finished pieces can be displayed in a school display case. Students can write the name of the person and his or her birth and death dates on an index card to display beside their monuments in the display case.

The Vietnam Women's Memorial
(Cornerstones of Freedom)

Deborah Kent
(Chicago: Children's Press, 1995)

Book Summary: Thirteen thousand women served in the Vietnam War as nurses, air traffic controllers, intelligence officers, mapmakers, and clerks. This picture book describes the personal stories of several women who experienced the war, the reactions of the American people upon their return, and their efforts to gain approval for a Vietnam Women's memorial in Washington, D.C.

Key Concepts: Women, Vietnam War

National History Standards: 4 and 7

Anticipation/Reaction Guide

The Vietnam Women's Memorial

Before   **After**

_____   1. The US was involved in the Vietnam War in Southeast Asia   _____
                between 1965 and 1973.

_____   2. The US attempted to defeat the communist North Vietnamese.   _____

_____   3. Approximately 6,000 women served in the Vietnam War.   _____

_____   4. Many women who served in Vietnam were nurses, caring for   _____
                servicemen and Vietnamese children.

_____   5. Everyone in the US treated both men and women soldiers as heroes _____
                when they returned to America from the war.

_____   6. Diane Carlson Evans, a nurse who served in the Vietnam War,   _____
                initiated the idea of a memorial for the women who had served.

_____   7. The government immediately liked the idea of a Vietnam Women's _____
                Memorial and quickly gave approval for its placement near the
                Vietnam Veterans' War Memorial in Washington, D.C.

_____   8. Presidents Jimmy Carter, Ronald Reagan, and George H. W. Bush _____
                participated in the authorization and placement of the new memorial.

_____   9. The Commission on Fine Arts did not like the original design   _____
                for the statue, so a nationwide competition was held.

_____   10. Vice President Al Gore delivered the keynote address at the   _____
                dedication ceremony on Veterans Day, November 11, 1993.

Source: http://www.ncrel.org/sdrs/areas/issues/students/learning/lr1anti.htm

Activity #1: Anticipation/Reaction Guide

Materials for Activity #1:
- Anticipation/reaction guide (1 per student; see handout)

Areas of Integration: Making predictions, listening skills, oral expression

Before reading *The Vietnam Women's Memorial*, give each student an anticipation/reaction guide. Ask them to complete the "before" column by writing true or false beside each statement. Encourage them to take their best guesses, even if they are not sure. Discuss guesses with students and have them explain why they chose the answer they did. Then read the book. As students listen to the story, they are to write true or false in the answer column. Have students compare their predictions with the correct answers.

Anticipation/Reaction Guide Answers

1. True
2. True
3. False. Approximately 13,000 American women served in Vietnam.
4. True
5. False. None of the soldiers from the Vietnam War received a hero's welcome when they returned.
6. True
7. False. It was very difficult to gain approval from the government for the Vietnam Women's Memorial.
8. False. Presidents Ronald Reagan and George H. Bush participated in the authorization and placement of the new memorial.
9. True
10. True

Activity #2: News Telecast of the Vietnam Women's Memorial Dedication

Materials for Activity #2:
- Writing paper (1 sheet per group)
- Props for news telecast (microphone, news desk)
- Video camera

Areas of Integration: Dramatic expression, written expression, cooperative learning

After reading and discussing the book, divide students into small groups. Ask them to write a television news report of the dedication of the Vietnam Women's Memorial. Edit each group's rough draft and provide suggestions for additions or changes. Have each group decide the roles that they will play in the telecast (news anchor, on-site reporter, Vice President Al Gore, Diane Carlson Evans, camera person, etc.). Allow groups time to rehearse their telecasts before they perform in front of the class. Videotape the telecasts so that group members can watch their performances and share it with family members.

Activity #3: Website Activities for Women in Vietnam

> **Materials for Activity #3:**
> • Internet access

Areas of Integration: Computer skills, written expression

After reading and discussing *The Vietnam Women's Memorial*, access the Vietnam Women's Memorial Project website at http://www.vietnamwomensmemorial.org/pages/index2.html. Choose from the following activities:

1. Have students watch the introductory movie and read the history of the Vietnam Women's Memorial. Ask them to compare the information from the book with that found on the website.

2. Have students read the newspaper articles that were written on the day of the dedication ceremony in 1993. Ask them to compare their television newscasts with the information in the newspaper articles. Discuss any new information that they learned from reading the articles.

3. Read and discuss the most frequently asked questions about the memorial.

4. Have students write the questions that they have about the role of women in the Vietnam War and send them to the contact persons listed on the website.

5. Request an interview with a woman who served in the Vietnam War. Interview requests can be sent to vwmpdc@aol.com.

6. Link to the Women at War website at http://tlc.discovery.com/tlcpages.vietnam.stories.htm. and have students watch the video clips of stories and interviews of women who served in Vietnam.

The Vietnam War (20th Century Perspectives)

Douglas Willoughby
(Chicago: Heinemann Library, 2001)

Book Summary: This book, a historical account of the Vietnam War, recounts background information, the United States' involvement in the war, the antiwar movement, the eventual collapse of South Vietnam, and changing public opinion regarding US involvement.

Key Concepts: Vietnam, Vietnam War, civil war, Communist, communism, North Vietnamese Army (NVA), Vietcong, napalm, refugees, guerrilla war, capitalist, Cold War, domino theory, grenade, Gulf of Tonkin Resolution, blockading, Agent Orange, herbicide, draft, platoon, UNESCO, pacifist, Pentagon, CIA

National History Standards: 4 and 7

Activity #1: Vietnam War Debate

Materials for Activity #1:
- Resource books on the Vietnam War or Internet access
- Note cards
- Pencils

Areas of Integration: Reading, writing, critical thinking, persuasive speaking, cooperative learning, research skills

After reading *The Vietnam War*, discuss the controversy that swelled around the United States' involvement in the Vietnam War. Divide students into two teams in order to conduct a debate of the subject. One team will support US involvement; the other team will oppose it. Have students further investigate the controversy by researching the topic in resource books and/or through information found on the Internet. They will record supporting information on index cards. Encourage each group to work as a cooperative team in organizing for the debate. The teacher or a volunteer student can serve as moderator for the debate. A typical time frame and a sequence of presentations for a debate are suggested below:

First group, pro position of the issue	3–5 minutes
First group, con position of the issue	3–5 minutes
Second group, pro position of the issue	3–5 minutes
Second group, con position of the issue	3–5 minutes
First group's rebuttal (con position)	1–2 minutes

First group's rebuttal (pro position)	1–2 minutes
Second group's rebuttal (con position)	1–2 minutes
Second group's rebuttal (pro position)	1–2 minutes

Activity #2: Vietnam War Word Wall

Materials for Activity #2:
- Sentence strips
- Markers
- Masking tape

Areas of Integration: Writing, speaking, vocabulary

Before reading the book, tell students that they will be creating a Vietnam War word wall within the classroom. Designate a wall space within the classroom for this purpose. Assemble markers and cut sentence strips onto which students can write key vocabulary terms from the book. Tell students that they will be using the words on the word wall for other related activities.

Prior to reading the book, ask students to listen for key vocabulary terms. As students identify them, have them print the terms on sentence strips, orally define them, and affix them to the classroom word wall in alphabetical order. Students can check the correctness of their definitions by comparing them with the definitions supplied in the book's glossary. Appropriate letter headings can be made for each word category. The following terms that should be included on the word wall:

Agent Orange	indicted
amphetamine	malaria
antipersonnel bombs	mangrove
ARVN	napalm
blockade	NLF
capitalism	NVA
CIA	pacifist
civil war	pardoned
Cold War	Pentagon
collective farms	platoon
Communist	Pulitzer Prize
dioxin	Quaker
domino theory	reeducation
draft	refugees
grenade	Returned and Services League
guerrilla war	trip-wire
Gulf of Tonkin Resolution	UNESCO
herbicide	Vietcong
hippie	Vietnam

After students have finished reading the book, defining the terms, and creating the word wall, have them each write a summary of what they have learned. The summary should include at least ten of the terms from the word wall. Students can share their summaries in class.

Activity #3: Historical Figure Attribute Web

Materials for Activity #3:

- Resource books or Internet access
- Chart paper (1 sheet per group)
- Markers (1 per group)

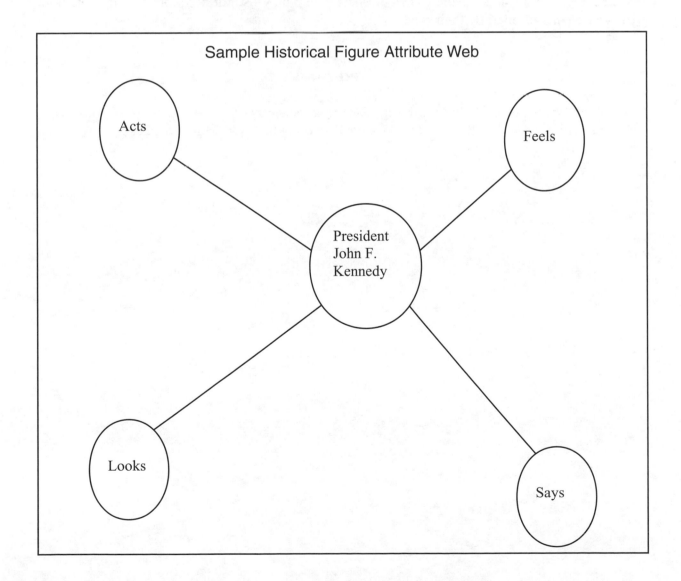

Sample Historical Figure Attribute Web

Acts

Feels

President John F. Kennedy

Looks

Says

Areas of Integration: Reading, writing, research skills, creative thinking, cooperative group work, speaking

After reading the book, write the following names from the book on the chalkboard:

President Harry S. Truman
President Dwight D. Eisenhower
President John F. Kennedy
President Lyndon B. Johnson
General William Westmoreland

Lieutenant William Calley
Martin Luther King, Jr.
President Richard M. Nixon
Daniel Ellsberg
Henry Kissinger

Students should then be grouped into pairs or small groups to create attribute webs for a selected figure from the list above. On chart paper, ask students to print the name of the person at the center of the web. Tell students to draw four branches from the center: acts, feels, looks, and says. Together, students can brainstorm a list of appropriate words and phrases for each of the above attributes using the book and other information gained from resource books and Internet searches, in making their attribute lists. They may use direct quotes from sources or write statements implied by their readings.

Related Books

Patrick-Wexler, D. *Colin Powell.* Austin, TX: Steck-Vaughn, 1996.
Zeinert, K. *The Valiant Women of the Vietnam War.* Brookfield, CT: Millbrook, 2000.

CHAPTER *10*

Women in History

All by Herself: 14 Girls Who Made a Difference

Ann Whitford Paul
(New York: Harcourt, 1999)

Book Summary: *All by Herself* is a collection of insightful poems about the girlhoods of both well-known and little-known women. The accomplishments, bravery, courage, and heroism of women such as Amelia Earhart, Pocahontas, and Rachel Carson can help students realize the significant differences made by females in the lives of others.

Key Concepts: Women in history, courage

National History Standards: 1, 4, and 6

Activity #1: Comparing School Experiences with Mary Jane McLeod Bethune

> **Materials for Activity #1:**
> - Writing paper (1 sheet per student)
> - Pre-writing activity sheet (1 per student; see handout)

Areas of Integration: Creative writing, comparing and contrasting

After reading and discussing the poem "Mary Jane McLeod" in *All by Herself*, encourage students to consider what Mary Jane's early school experiences were like. Allow them to discuss what her family thought about her attending school, what her school was like, whether she liked school, and how she learned to read. Students may want to read the 1996 issue of *Cobblestone* magazine and the children's books *She Wanted to Read: The Story of Mary McLeod Bethune* by Ella Carruth (Abingdon Press, 1966*), Mary McLeod Bethune: A Photo-Illustrated*

Pre-Writing Activity Sheet

Comparing School Experiences with Mary Jane McLeod Bethune

My School
(Describe building, location, first classroom, first teacher)

Mary Jane's School
(Describe building, location, first classroom, first teacher)

What I Think about School

What Mary Jane Thought about School

How I Learned to Read

How Mary Jane Learned to Read

Biography by Margo McLoone (Bridgestone, 1997), or *Building a Dream: Mary Bethune's School* (Stories of America) by Richard Kelso (Raintree/Steck-Vaughn, 1996), or websites such as www.lkwdpl.org/wihohio/beth-mar.htm, web.nypl.org/research/sc/scl/Bethune.html, or www.nahe.org/HAHC/Val/Columns/SC10-6.html to get more information. Ask students to compare their early school experiences and the way they learned to read with Mary Jane experiences by completing the pre-writing activity sheet. Students can then transfer their ideas into three paragraphs, comparing and contrasting their school experiences with Mary Jane's.

Activity #2: Literature Graffiti

Materials for Activity #2:

- Large pieces of newsprint
- Markers (1 per student)
- Tape

Areas of Integration: Critical thinking, written expression, expressive language

After reading and discussing the poem "Mary Jane McLeod" in *All by Herself*, allow students to consider what their lives might be like if they traded places with Mary Jane McLeod Bethune. Create sentence stems (see below) and put each one on a large piece of newsprint. Tape or attach the newsprint at various places on the walls of the classroom. Divide students into the same number of groups as there are sentence stems. Have each group go to one of the sentence stems. Give each group one minute to finish its sentence stem. All group members must write at the same time, so that no one has time to read or think about anyone else's response. At the end of one minute, the groups rotate around the room to the next sentence stem. The process continues until all groups have reacted to all sentence stems. Have the groups rotate through the sentence stems a second time so that students can read each other's responses. To process the activity, have each group stop at one sentence stem. Give the groups three or four minutes to summarize the reactions for that sentence stem in one or two sentences. Have each group write its summary at the bottom of the reactions or on a new piece of paper. Ask each group to select a spokesperson(s) to share its summary with the class. Ask students for reactions and comments.

Possible sentence stems include the following

If I didn't know how to read . . .

If I had to walk five miles each way to school . . .

If I weren't allowed to go to school . . .

If I worked really hard at school . . .

If I had to study by candlelight . . .

If I were Mary Jane McLeod . . .

Source: Adapted from Rose-Colley, Bechtel, & Cinelli (1994).

Activity #3: Analysis of Quotes from Mary McLeod Bethune/Service Project

---

Materials for Activity #3:
- Writing paper (1 sheet per group)

Areas of Integration: Critical thinking, expressive language, written expression

After reading and discussing the poem "Mary Jane McLeod" in *All by Herself*, ask students to consider the following quotes from Mary McLeod Bethune:

"Not for myself, but for others."

"I feel that as I give, I get."

"From the first, I made my learning, what little it was, useful every way I could."

"Faith is the first factor in a life devoted to service. Without it, nothing is possible. With it, nothing is impossible."

Place students in groups of three or four and ask them to discuss each quote. Provide them with the following questions to guide their discussion:

What do you think was important in Mary McLeod Bethune's life? Why?

How do you think she developed these qualities?

What quote do you identify most with and why?

How do you make your learning useful?

Have you done anything that is of service to others? If so, what? If so, how did it make you feel?

A representative from each group may want to jot down the reactions to each question so that they can be shared with the class. Have students think about a service project that the class might do in the classroom, school, or community. Encourage students to start small and ensure that all class members become involved. Ideas for service projects could include a peer tutoring project with a lower grade, a gardening project on school grounds or in the community, or a food drive for a homeless shelter.

A Picture Book of Sojourner Truth

David Adler
(New York: Scholastic, 1994)

Book Summary: This picture book tells the story of a slave girl named Isabella. When she gained her freedom she changed her name to Sojourner Truth, because she wanted to move about and preach the truth. Sojourner was one of the first African-American women to win a lawsuit against a white man. She traveled thousands of miles across the United States to speak out against slavery.

Key Concepts: Slavery, women in history

National History Standards: 4 and 6

Activity #1: Create a Flannel-Board Scene

> **Materials for Activity #1:**
> - Flannel board
> - Felt sheets of different colors
> - Glue
> - Scissors
> - Markers

Areas of Integration: Creative and artistic expression, oral language

After reading *A Picture Book of Sojourner Truth*, divide students into small groups. Have each group choose a scene from the book to retell using flannel-board characters. Each group must:

1. Rewrite the scene with both narrator and characters' parts

2. Determine who will be the narrator and who will be each of the characters

3. Draw the characters and props on felt and cut them out

4. Practice placing the characters and props on the flannel board while retelling the story

5. Perform the scene for the class

If time allows, permit each group to make its own flannel board. Give each group a two-pocket folder and have students glue a piece of felt on the outside, covering the entire folder. Bend the folder in the middle so that it stands up, with the felt side facing the group. Students can now practice their flannel-board stories in small groups. The pockets in the folder can be used to hold the flannel-board pieces.

Activity #2: Make a Bookmark

> **Materials for Activity #2:**
>
> • Bookmarks cut from poster board
> • Magazines
> • Scraps of material, felt, and so on
> • Glue and scissors
> • Markers, crayons, and paints

Areas of Integration: Artistic expression, oral language

After reading and discussing *A Picture Book of Sojourner Truth*, give each student a blank bookmark. Ask them to use magazine pictures, scraps of materials, and other art supplies to create a bookmark that represents the life and contributions of Sojourner Truth. Encourage creativity and innovative ways of representing her strengths. In small groups, ask students to share their bookmarks.

Activity #3: Anticipation/Reaction Guides for Sojourner Truth

> **Materials for Activity #3:**
>
> • Anticipation/reaction guides
> (1 per student; see handout)

Areas of Integration: Critical thinking, auditory memory

Before reading *A Picture Book of Sojourner Truth*, give each student an anticipation/reaction guide. Students are to read each statement and write *yes* in the *Before* column if they believe the statement is true and *no* in the *Before* column if they believe the statement is false. Read the book to the students. Have the students now write *yes* or *no* in the *After* column for each statement based on what they learned from the story.

Anticipation/Reaction Guide

A Picture Book of Sojourner Truth

Before	*After*	
_____	_____	1. Sojourner Truth's name at birth was Isabella Baumfree.
_____	_____	2. Sojourner Truth was born into slavery.
_____	_____	3. There were no states that granted freedom to slaves prior to the end of the Civil War.
_____	_____	4. Sojourner Truth was one of the first African-American women to win a lawsuit against a white man.
_____	_____	5. Sojourner traveled to foreign lands to speak out against slavery.
_____	_____	6. Sojourner raised money during the Civil War to help feed African-American slaves.
_____	_____	7. During the Civil War, Sojourner got an opportunity to meet with President Andrew Johnson.
_____	_____	8. Sojourner helped obtain equal privileges for African Americans in Arlington, Virginia.
_____	_____	9. Sojourner's proposal to provide western land to freed slaves so that they could support themselves was not supported by Congress.
_____	_____	10. Freed slaves soon found work and were able to support themselves and their families.

Source: http://www.ncrel.org/sdrs/areas/issues/students/learning/lr1anti.htm

Answers for Anticipation/Reaction Guide

1. After: Yes

2. After: Yes

3. After: No

4. After: Yes

5. After: No

6. After: Yes

7. After: No

8. After: Yes

9. After: Yes

10. After: No

Maya Angelou: Greeting the Morning

Sarah King
(Brookfield, CT: Millbrook Press, 1994)

Book Summary: This biographical account of Maya Angelou describes the life and many outstanding accomplishments of the talented black writer. The book describes her triumph over many personal difficulties to become the second poet in American history to deliver an inaugural poem. The book begins with her birth in Saint Louis, Missouri, in 1928 and concludes with her historic delivery of her poem "On the Pulse of Morning" at the 1993 inauguration of President William J. Clinton.

Key Concepts: Apartheid, Civil Rights movement, Jim Crow laws, racism, segregation, inauguration

National History Standards: 1, 2, 3, 4, and 7

Activity #1: Maya Angelou: A Résumé of Success

Materials for Activity #1:
- Sample résumé, printed on chart paper or overhead transparencies
- Overhead projector
- Résumé forms (1 per student; see handout)
- Internet access
- Pencils

Résumé for Maya Angelou

Name:

Birth date:

Birthplace:

Life's Goal(s):

Educational background (include dates, if known):

Work experience (include dates, if known):

Publications:

Books:

Poems:

Distinctions and honors (include dates, if known):

Areas of Integration: Reading, writing, oral skills

After reading the story, show students a sample of a résumé. Ask them: What is a résumé? Who has a résumé? What kind of information is found on a résumé? When might a person create a résumé? Do all résumés look alike? Do all résumés contain the same information? Why or why not?

After discussing résumés, ask students to create a résumé for Maya Angelou using the résumé form provided and the biographical information contained in the book. If necessary, students can use the Internet to obtain more details about Angelou's life.

After résumés have been completed, students can share them in class and compare the facts that they have incorporated into their résumés for Maya Angelou.

Activity #2: It's All in the Name

Materials for Activity #2:

- Name reference book or Internet access
- White construction paper
- Crayons, markers, colored pencils
- Scissors

Areas of Integration: Creative and artistic expression, research skills, reading, writing, oral language

After reading the book, have students recall Maya Angelou's birth name, Marguerite Johnson. Discuss how and why she changed her name (it was her brother Bailey's special nickname for her) and the meaning of the name "Maya" ("my sister").

Using name reference books or the Internet, have students research their own first names to find out what they mean. After discovering the meanings of their names, have students design a nameplate for themselves, using white construction paper, crayons, markers, and colored pencils. They might want to cut the nameplates into the first letter of their names or into the shape of the object their name represents. (For example, the name Deborah means "the bee.") Encourage them to include the following information on their creative nameplates: original name, origin of name, meaning of name, and other anecdotal information that they can find relating to their names.

After the nameplates are complete, have students share them in class. Attach completed nameplates to students' desks for display or on their lockers or cubbies.

Activity #3: Dear Abby—It's Me, Maya

> **Materials for Activity #3:**
> - A sample "Dear Abby" letter from a newspaper
> - Composition paper
> - Pencils

Areas of Integration: Reading, creative writing, letter formatting, critical and creative thinking, oral speaking

After reading the book, discuss with students the many problems encountered by Maya Angelou throughout her lifetime (examples: being sent to live with her grandmother at the age of three, segregation and prejudice, being assaulted by her mother's friend, being separated from her brother Bailey, her many jobs). List student examples on the chalkboard.

Following this, share with students a letter from the "Dear Abby" column of the newspaper. After reading the letter, have students discuss appropriate responses to the letter that was read. After students have responded, share the newspaper response with them.

Divide students into pairs. Tell them that they are going to write letters to Dear Abby as if they were Maya Angelou seeking advice on how to handle one of her problems. One student in the pair will compose the letter; the other student will compose the response to the letter. Have students share letters and responses in class. Other students can suggest possible, alternative responses to the problems being expressed. Students might even choose to role-play the problems and solutions in class.

Related Books

Adler, D. *A Picture Book of Harriet Tubman.* New York: Scholastic, 1982.

———. *A Picture Book of Helen Keller.* New York: Trumpet Club, 1990.

Atkins, J. *Mary Anning and the Sea Dragon.* New York: Farrar Straus Giroux, 1999.

Bains, R. *Clara Barton: Angel of the Battlefield.* Mahwah, NJ: Troll, 1982.

Brown, D. *Alice Ramsey's Grand Adventure.* Boston: Houghton Mifflin, 1997.

Cooney, B. *Eleanor.* New York: Puffin, 1996.

Corey, S. *You Forgot Your Skirt, Amelia Bloomer.* New York: Scholastic, 2000.

Dungworth, R., and P. Wingate. *Famous Women: From Nefertiti to Diana.* New York: Scholastic, 1996.

Haven, K. *Amazing American Women: Forty Fascinating 5-Minute Reads.* Greenwood Village, CO: Teacher Ideas Press, 1995.

Lasky, K. *Vision of Beauty: The Story of Sarah Breedlove Walker.* Cambridge, MA: Candlewick, 2000.

Matthews, G. *American Women's History: A Student Companion.* New York: Oxford University Press, 2000.

McKissack, P., P. McKissack, and F. McKissack. *Sojourner Truth: Ain't I A Woman?* New York: Scholastic, 1994.

Ryan, P. *Amelia and Eleanor Go for a Ride.* New York: Scholastic, 1999.

Sabin, F. *Amelia Earhart: Adventure in the Sky.* Mahwah, NJ: Troll, 1983.

———. *The Courage of Helen Keller.* Mahwah, NJ: Troll, 1982.

Zeldis, M. *Sisters in Strength: American Women Who Made a Difference.* New York: Henry Holt, 2000.

CHAPTER **11**

Men in History

Duke Ellington

Andrea Pinkney
(New York: Hyperion, 1998)

Book Summary: This Caldecott Honor and Coretta Scott King award-winning book tells the story of piano great Duke Ellington. Born Edward Kennedy Ellington in 1899 in Washington, D.C., Ellington was not impressed with the sound of the piano when he was a youngster. In fact, he quit his piano lessons while he was a young child. It was not until years later that he gained a new respect for the musical instrument. He and his band got the big break that they needed in 1927 when they were asked to play at Harlem's most famous nightspot, the Cotton Club. Ellington, nicknamed "King of the Keys," died on May 24, 1974, leaving behind him a musical legacy that will long live on in the history of music.

Key Concepts: Jazz, ragtime music, Harlem, Creole, jambalaya, Carnegie Hall

National History Standards: 6 and 7

Activity #1: Literally and Figuratively Speaking

> **Materials for Activity #1:**
> • White construction paper (1 per student)
> • Crayons, marker, and colored pencils
> • Pencils
> • Hole punch
> • 3 brass fasteners

Areas of Integration: Creative and critical thinking, reading, writing, artistic expression, figurative language, speaking

The book *Duke Ellington* is rich in figurative language. Begin by discussing the difference between literal and figurative language with the class. Use common examples to discuss the difference between what the expression says literally, and the figurative interpretations of each. Consider and discuss the following examples:

I'm so hungry, I could eat a horse.

It is raining cats and dogs.

He is always putting his foot in his own mouth.

Sally is a two-faced person.

Following the discussion, divide students into pairs to illustrate figurative expressions found in the book. One student will write the expression and illustrate it in a literal, humorous way. The student's partner will write and illustrate the translation of the phrase. Students can choose from the following examples from the book:

"the man with the cats who could swing with his band"

he "kissed the piano a fast good-bye"

"Duke's fingers rode the piano keys"

"He had fine-as-pie looks and flashy threads"

"But soon they split the D.C. scene and made tracks for New York"

"for Harlem, the place where jazz music ruled"

"Lady Luck smiled pretty on the Washingtonians"

"folks dreamed of sitting pretty at the Cotton [Club]"

"sometimes the Orchestra performed the tunes straight-up"

"make the music fly"

"each instrument raised its own voice"

"one by one, each cat took the floor and wiped it clean with his own special way of playing"

"his gut bucket tunes put a spell on the room"

"yeah, those solos were kickin' "

"hot-buttered bop"

"Slide me some King of the Keys, please."

"Billy became Duke's ace"

"Outside, the winter wind was cold and slapping"

"Carnegie Hall was sizzling with applause"

When students have finished, ask them to share their literal and figurative interpretations in class. Collect student work and create a class collaboration book by punching three holes down the left side and fastening pages with brass fasteners. Have students create a title page and an author page for the book as well.

Activity #2: A Song and Dance to Duke

> **Materials for Activity #2:**
> - Composition paper
> - Pencils

Areas of Integration: Creative expression, creative movement, lyrical rhythm, writing

After reading the book, divide students into small groups to create originals songs or creative dances that tell about the life of Duke Ellington. If students are creating a song, they might choose to write their words to a familiar lyric such as "Twinkle, Twinkle Little Star," "Row, Row, Row Your Boat," or any other tune with which they are familiar. Students should include information provided in the book in their song or dance. Students can then perform their songs and dances for the class.

Activity #3: What a Movie! . . . or . . . What? A Movie?

> **Materials for Activity #3:**
> - Composition paper
> - Pencils

Areas of Integration: Critical thinking, creative writing, reading, speaking

After reading the book, ask students to consider whether they think the book *Duke Ellington* would make a good movie. You might discuss other movies they have seen about famous musicians, athletes, or movie stars. Ask them: What made that movie good or bad?

Have each student take a stance on the issue and create a position paper that supports his or her view. Encourage them to use specific examples from the book and Duke Ellington's life.

When students are finished, they can share their papers in class and compare and contrast opinions expressed by the class. As a follow-up activity, students might even research the Internet in order to find out whether a movie was ever produced about the life of Duke Ellington.

More Than Anything Else

Marie Bradby
(New York: Orchard, 1995)

Book Summary: More than anything else, nine-year-old Booker T. Washington wants to learn how to read. He spends his days shoveling salt at the saltworks of Malden, West Virginia, with his father and older brother, John. One day, young Booker hears a man reading a newspaper aloud to others in his town and is further inspired to learn how to read. With a small blue book his mother gives him, he seeks out the man and learns "the song—the sounds the marks [in the book] make." Booker learns to read and later shares this gift with others who also long to read.

Key Concepts: Saltworks, Kanawha River, literacy

National History Standards: 1, 2, 3, and 7

Activity #1: Calling All Volunteers: Be a Buddy Reader

> **Materials for Activity #1:**
> - Books (selected by students)
> - Poems (selected by students)

Areas of Integration: Volunteerism, community service, oral expression, interpersonal skills

Booker T. Washington wanted to learn how to read. Discuss with students the fact that many people are not able to read due to a variety of reasons, such as poverty, lack of education, handicaps, or serious illness.

Contact local agencies, such as the town library, hospital, and retirement homes to volunteer students to read to others. Have students select appropriate books and poems that can be shared with their buddies. You might even want to take photographs of the buddy readers and create a community service bulletin board to display at school.

Activity #2: Before and After Character Sketches

> **Materials for Activity #2:**
>
> • Chart paper
> • Markers
> • Composition paper
> • Pencils

Areas of Integration: Reading, writing, using adjectives, critical thinking

Before reading *More Than Anything Else*, ask students to listen for words that describe Booker T. Washington during the first half of the book. Explain that the words that describe people and objects are called adjectives. While reading the first half of the book, record student responses on chart paper. Pause and discuss each adjective and ask students for evidence from the book that directly states or implies that Washington was this way.

Continue reading the second half of the book, having students describe Washington after he learns how to read. List these on a separate sheet of chart paper and ask students to give evidence that supports their answers from the book.

After finishing the book, have students compare Washington before and after he learned how to read. Ask them: Was he a different person? How so?

Ask students to reflect on their own lives and think about an event that changed them in some significant way. Have them list five adjectives that described them before the event and five adjectives that described them after the event. Ask students to write a short story telling about the event that changed their lives. Students can choose whether they want to share their stories in class or keep them private.

Activity #3: My Time Capsule

> **Materials for Activity #3:**
>
> • Shoe boxes or large envelopes (1 per student), brought in by students
> • Artifacts that represent a student's life (brought in by students)
> • A Booker T. Washington Time Capsule (shoe box) that contains the following items:
>
> | | |
> |---|---|
> | a small bag of salt | a rubber frog |
> | a newspaper | a candle |
> | a book | a stick |
> | stencils of the alphabet | |

Areas of Integration: Critical and creative thinking, oral language

Before reading the book, ask students what a time capsule is. Explain that a time capsule contains a collection of artifacts and objects that represent a person in a particular period in history. Show students the objects in the Booker T. Washington time capsule, one at a time, and ask them to predict how the objects in the time capsule might relate to a person's life. Ask them: What could the candle be used for? What could the salt represent? What might the stick represent?

Following the discussion of the objects in the time capsule, introduce the book *More Than Anything Else*. Tell students to listen to the story in order to find out what the objects represent and why they might have been included in the time capsule. After reading the book, discuss the significance of each item.

Next, have students reflect on their own lives and the objects that might best represent themselves in a time capsule. Ask students to construct secret shoebox time capsules at home and bring them to class. Tell them not to share the contents with anyone else, since students will be examining the time capsules at school and guessing to whom each belongs. Students should include at least ten items, which must all fit within a shoebox. Suggest items that they might include, such as a photograph, a vacation memento, a favorite book or poem, or an item from a sport or hobby.

After the time capsules arrive at school, number each and set them up in a display area of the classroom. Have students circulate, examine the contents of each, and guess to whom each belongs. After students record their predictions, have each student share his or her time capsule with the class and explain the significance of each item. Audience members can check to see how many students they guessed correctly.

A Picture Book of George Washington Carver

David Adler
(New York: Holiday House, 1999)

Book Summary: This book focuses on the life and accomplishments of George Washington Carver. Born into slavery on a Missouri farm near the end of the Civil War, Carver was the son of slaves. While he was still an infant, he and his mother were kidnapped by raiders and taken to Arkansas. A neighbor found the boy, but not his mother, and he returned him safely to the farm of Moses and Susan Carver who raised George and his brother, James. The book also describes Carver's work with finding new uses for peanut by-products and sweet potatoes. After living a life dedicated to improving the lives of Southern African Americans, Carver died on January 5, 1943.

Key Concepts: Slave, Civil War, Ku Klux Klan, lynching, persecution, agriculture, agriculturalist, by-products, Thomas Alva Edison, National Association for the Advancement of Colored People

National History Standards: 3, 6, 7, and 8

Activity #1: Our Favorite Peanut and Sweet Potato Recipes

Materials for Activity #1:

- Recipes using sweet potatoes or peanuts
(brought in by students)
- Hole punch
- 3 brass fasteners

Areas of Integration: Reading, writing, word processing

George Washington Carver discovered more than 300 different uses for peanuts and more than 100 useful products made from sweet potatoes. After discussing some of the products Washington discovered from these two food items, ask students to bring to class a favorite recipe that uses either peanuts or sweet potatoes. Students can word process their recipes and create illustrations for them. Recipes can be collected and compiled into a class Peanut and Sweet Potato Recipe Book. If possible, students could bring samples of the foods to class, and students could have a taste-testing party to sample other students' favorite recipes.

Activity #2: George Washington Carver: A Monologue in History

Materials for Activity #2:

- Composition paper
- Pencils
- Resource books on George Washington Carver
or Internet access

Areas of Integration: Reading, writing, speaking, research skills

After reading the book, have students discuss the life of George Washington Carver and his many interests. Discuss his early life and the events surrounding his parents' disappearances. Discuss his early education and the lynching he witnessed while he was a young man. Finally, discuss his life as a farmer, scholar, artist, humanitarian, scientist, and inventor.

Have students create a written monologue for Carver that reflects his life as a black child, farmer, scholar, artist, humanitarian, scientist, or inventor. Students can dress as that character and present their monologues before the class.

Activity #3: Create-a-Board Game

> **Materials for Activity #3:**
>
> - Poster board (1 per group)
> - Construction paper (varied colors)
> - Crayons, makers, and colored pencils
> - Glue (1 per group)
> - $3'' \times 5''$ index cards
> - Scissors
> - George Washington Carver resource books or Internet access
> - Pencils

Areas of Integration: Reading, writing, creative thinking, artistic expression

After reading and discussing the book, divide students into small groups of four or five and ask them to create a board game based on the life of George Washington Carver. Encourage students to use facts about Carver's life in creating the questions for the game cards. The book can be used as a primary source of information, or students can research Carver further via the Internet or resource books. They will use a large piece of poster board to create the game board and write game questions on $3'' \times 5''$ index cards. Students might choose peanuts as game pieces or some other symbolic item that represents Carver.

In addition to creating the game board, groups are responsible for writing specific instructions for how the game is played. When students are done with their games, they can share them and explain them to the class. Students can then take turns playing each other's games.

Related Books

Adler, D. *A Picture Book of Abraham Lincoln*. New York: Scholastic, 1989.
———. *A Picture Book of Benjamin Franklin*. New York: Trumpet Club, 1990.
———. *A Picture Book of Christopher Columbus*. New York: Trumpet Club, 1991.
———. *A Picture Book of George Washington*. New York: Scholastic, 1989.
———. *A Picture Book of John F. Kennedy*. New York: Scholastic, 1991.
———. *A Picture Book of Martin Luther King, Jr.* New York: Scholastic, 1989.
Bains, R. *James Monroe: Young Patriot*. Mahwah, NJ: Troll, 1986.
Brandt, K. *Lou Gehrig: Pride of the Yankees*. Mahwah, NJ: Troll, 1986.
Brenner, M. *Abe Lincoln's Hat*. New York: Scholastic, 1994.
Denengerg, B. *Nelson Mandela: No Easy Walk to Freedom*. New York: Scholastic, 1991.
———. *Stealing Home: A Story of Jackie Robinson*. New York: Scholastic, 1997.
Frady, M. *Jesse Jackson: A Biography*. New York: Random House, 1996.
Haskins, J. *One More River to Cross: The Story of Twelve Black Americans*. New York: Scholastic, 1992.
Krull, K. *Lives of the Presidents: Fame, Shame (and What the Neighbors Thought)*. New York: Scholastic, 1998.

Lord, B. *In The Year of the Boar and Jackie Robinson*. New York: Scholastic, 1984.

Lovitt, C. *Michael Jordan*. New York: Scholastic, 1998.

MacLeod, E. *Alexander Graham Bell: An Inventive Life*. New York: Scholastic, 1999.

Mattern, J. *Young Martin Luther King, Jr.: I Have a Dream*. Mahwah, NJ: Troll, 1992.

McGovern, A. *If You Grew Up with Abraham Lincoln*. New York: Scholastic, 1966.

McKissack, P., and F. McKissack. *Black Diamond: The Story of the Negro Baseball Leagues*. New York: Scholastic,

Myers, W. D. *Malcolm X: By Any Means Necessary: A Biography*. New York: Scholastic, 1999.

Pinkney, A. *Dear Benjamin Banneker*. San Diego, CA: Harcourt Brace, 1994.

Ransome, L. *Satchel Paige*. Riverdale, NJ: Simon & Schuster, 2000.

Reef, C. *Paul Laurence Dunbar: Portrait of a Poet*. African-American Biographies Series. Berkeley Heights, NJ: Enslow, 2000.

Spencer, L. *NBA Superstar Shaquille O'Neal*. NBA Reader. New York: Scholastic, 2002.

Troupe, Q. *Take It to the Hoop, Magic Johnson*. New York: Hyperion Press, 2000.

Related Poetry

Hopkins, Lee Bennett. "Dreamer." In *Lives: Poems about Famous Americans*. Ed. Lee Bennett Hopkins. New York: HarperCollins, 1999.

Schertle, Alice. "Abe." In *Lives: Poems about Famous Americans*. Ed. Lee Bennett Hopkins. New York: HarperCollins, 1999.

CHAPTER 12

Native Americans

Tallchief: America's Prima Ballerina

Maria Tallchief with Rosemary Wells
(New York: Viking, 1999)

Book Summary: This is the autobiography of Maria Tallchief, one of America's most famous ballerinas. Maria was born on an Osage Indian Reservation at a time when women were not allowed to dance. The story covers the family's move to Los Angeles so that Maria could attend ballet school, and her subsequent move to New York City to join the famous Ballets Russes de Monte Carlo.

Key Concepts: Native American history, ballet, career choice

National History Standards: 1, 4, and 6

Activity #1: Research Project

Materials for Activity #1:

- Internet and library resources
- Poster paper
- Mural paper
- Art supplies (markers, crayons, scraps of material)
- Dress-up clothes

Areas of Integration: Artistic and creative expression, creative dramatics, mathematics, oral language

After reading and discussing *Tallchief: America's Prima Ballerina*, ask students to use library and Internet resources to research the life of Maria Tallchief and her contributions to the arts. Encourage students to document their findings by choosing one of the following projects:

1. Create a time line of the events in Maria's life. Students may work individually or in small groups.

2. Create a poster or collage portraying Maria's ideas, interests, beliefs, and how she made a difference in the world of dance. Allow each student an opportunity to share and explain his or her artwork.

3. Dress up as Maria and prepare a short speech that explains the impact she had on diversity within the arts.

Activity #2: Simulated Interviews

Materials for Activity #2:
- Writing paper
- Microphone

Areas of Integration: Writing, creative dramatics, oral language

After reading the book, ask students to think about other things that they would like to know about Maria Tallchief. Ask students to develop interview questions that they would ask Maria if they had the opportunity. Have a student volunteer to play the role of Maria and simulate the interviews. (Students may want to give "Maria" their interview questions in advance so that "she" is prepared with historically accurate responses.)

Activity #3: Newscast from the Past

Materials for Activity #3:
- Microphone
- Dress-up clothes

Areas of Integration: Research skills, writing, creative dramatics, cooperative learning

After reading *Tallchief: America's Prima Ballerina*, divide students into small groups. Ask them to write and perform a "newscast from the past" depicting an event from this story or from any time in Maria's life. (Example: In tonight's news, Maria Tallchief . . .") All students in each group must participate in some way in the production of the newscast, and each group must decide who will be writers, newscasters, directors, and so on. In the newscast, students must include other events that were going on during this period in history.

A Picture Book of Sacagawea

David Adler
(New York: Scholastic, 2000)

Book Summary: Sacagawea was a Shoshone who was taken prisoner by a Hidatsa war tribe when she was a young girl. She was later sold to a white trader and trapper and became his second wife. Her husband became the interpreter for Meriwether Lewis and William Clark, and Sacagawea accompanied them on their expedition to the Pacific Ocean.

Key Concepts: Native American history, Lewis and Clark expedition, women in history

National History Standards: 1, 5, and 6

Activity #1: How Long Would It Take?

> **Materials for Activity #1:**
> - Map of the United States showing the Lewis and Clark route
> - Graph paper (1 piece per student)

Areas of Integration: Mathematical reasoning, map skills

After reading and discussing *A Picture Book of Sacagawea*, using a map of the United States, ask students to estimate the number of miles Sacagawea traveled with Lewis and Clark. Ask students to consider if it took seven to eight months to travel the route on foot, how long it would take

1. By car at 65 miles per hour?

2. By plane at 500 miles per hour?

3. By bicycle at 14 miles per hour?

After determining the length of time for each mode of travel, have students create a bar graph comparing the times required to reach the Pacific Ocean.

Activity #2: Sequence of Events

Materials for Activity #2:

• Sequence of Events sentences (1 sheet per student; see handout)
• Scissors
• Glue sticks

Areas of Integration: Auditory memory, sequencing skills

Before reading the book, pass out the Sequence of Events sheets. Allow students to cut out the sentences. As you read the book aloud, have students put the sentences in the order that they occurred in the story. To check their work, divide students into pairs to compare their answers. Discuss the correct order as a large group.

Sequence of Events

A Picture Book of Sacagawea

• Members of the expedition crossed the Continental Divide and met up with the Shoshone.

• Lewis and Clark and their men built Fort Mandan.

• Sacagawea was taken prisoner and her mother was killed.

• One explorer's boat turned on its side in a gust of wind, and Sacagawea saved the instruments and medicines.

• Sacagawea was sold to Toussaint Charbonneau, and she became his second wife.

• Rivers, lakes, and mountains have all been named for Sacagawea.

• When they reached the Pacific Ocean, Sacagawea was fascinated with a beached whale and the ocean.

• Sacagawea's baby, Jean Baptiste, was born.

• The explorers encountered wild animals on their trip and were often tired and hungry.

• President Thomas Jefferson sent Lewis and Clark to find a route to the Pacific Ocean.

Activity #3: Story Maps

> **Materials for Activity #3:**
> • Story Map sheets (1 per student; see handout)

Areas of Integration: Critical thinking, written expression

After reading and discussing *A Picture Book of Sacagawea*, have students complete a story map. Encourage students to think about the problem that was facing Lewis and Clark, and the role by played Sacagawea in its resolution.

The Legend of the Indian Paintbrush

Tomie dePaola
(New York: Paperstar, 1988)

Book Summary: The Indian Paintbrush is a red, orange, and yellow flower that grows throughout the Plains states. There are many stories related to the origin of the flower, and this Native American legend is one of them. Tomie dePaola tells of the gift of the Indian Paintbrush that Little Gopher brought to his people.

Key Concepts: Native American legends

National History Standards: 1 and 6

Activity #1: Tri-fold Book Summary

> **Materials for Activity #1:**
> • 8½″×11″ white paper (1 per student)
> • Markers, crayons

Areas of Integration: Listening skills, artistic expression, oral language

After reading and discussing *The Legend of the Indian Paintbrush*, give each student a sheet of white paper. Ask students to fold the paper in thirds. Discuss with students what they believe to be the main events at the beginning, the middle, and the end of the story. Then have

Story Map

Title:_____ Author:_____

Setting:

    Characters:

    Place:

    Time:

Problem:

Events Leading to Resolution:

1.

2.

3.

4.

Resolution:

students show on each of the three sections of paper what happened at the beginning, the middle, and the end of the story, in words and pictures. Allow students to take their drawings to a lower grade, pair each student with another child, and have them retell the story.

Activity #2: Make a Commercial

> **Materials for Activity #2:**
> • Writing paper (1 or 2 sheets per group)
> • Props
> • Videotaping equipment

Areas of Integration: Written expression, dramatic expression, cooperative learning

After reading and discussing the *The Legend of the Indian Paintbrush*, divide students into groups of three or four. Ask students to write a commercial advertising the book. Remind students that they are trying to "sell" the story to the class and could include a "jingle" if the group prefers. After commercials are written, have students act them out for the class. Commercials could be videotaped, so that the book could be "sold" to another class.

Activity #3: Totem Pole Books

> **Materials for Activity #3:**
> • Construction paper
> • Markers and crayons
> • Staplers

Areas of Integration: Written expression, artistic expression, oral language

After reading and discussing the sequence of events in *The Legend of the Indian Paintbrush*, have students create totem pole books detailing each section of the story. Students should draw or write about each of the main events in the story on a different color of construction paper. (For example, in a five-page book, the events might include 1. Little Gopher and his inability to keep up with the other children, 2. his visit with the wise shaman, 3. the dream vision that came to him, 4. his first paintings, 5. the brushes that turned into Indian Paintbrushes.) When the pages are complete, staple them together to make a book. Encourage students to share their books and the legend of the Indian Paintbrush with younger children.

Related Books

Bruchac, J. *Sacagawea*. San Diego, CA: Silver Whistle, 2000.
Cohlene, T. *Little Firefly: An Algonquian Legend*. Mahwah, NJ: Watermill Press, 1990.
DePaola, T. *The Legend of the Bluebonnett*. New York: G. P. Putnam's Sons, 1983.
Marrin, A. *Sitting Bull and His World*. New York: Dutton, 2000.
Smith, C. *Jingle Dancer*. New York: HarperCollins, 2000.

Related Poetry

Hopkins, Lee Bennett ed., "A Song for Sacagawea: Lewis and Clark Expedition, 1803–1806." In *Lives: Poems about Famous Americans*. New York: HarperCollins, 1999.

Appendix: National Standards for History

Standard 1: Students should be able to understand family life now and in the past; family life in various places long ago.

Standard 2: Students should be able to understand the history of their local community and how communities in North America varied long ago.

Standard 3: Students should be able to understand the people, events, problems, and ideas that created the history of their state.

Standard 4: Students should be able to understand how democratic values came to be and how they have been exemplified by people, events, and symbols.

Standard 5: Students should be able to understand the causes and nature of various movements of large groups of people into and within the United States, now and long ago.

Standard 6: Students should be able to understand regional folklore and cultural contributions that helped to form our national heritage.

Standard 7: Students should be able to understand selected attributes and historical developments of various societies in Africa, the Americas, Asia, and Europe.

Standard 8: Students should be able to understand major discoveries in science and technology, their social and economic effects, and the scientists and inventors responsible for them.

Source: National Center for History in the Schools. *National Standards for History*. Los Angeles, CA: University of California, 1996.

Books/Standards Matrix

This matrix outlines the history standards that are emphasized for each book title.

	1	2	3	4	5	6	7	8
Building a New Land: African-Americans in Colonial America	x				x	x		
Nickommoh! A Thanksgiving Celebration	x	x				x		
The First Thanksgiving	x	x		x	x	x		
I Have Heard of a Land	x	x	x	x	x		x	
Black Cowboy, Wild Horses					x	x		
Voices of the Alamo		x	x	x				
Sybil's Night Ride	x			x				

	1	2	3	4	5	6	7	8
The American Revolution (Voices in African-American History Series)				x		x		
Come All You Brave Soldiers: Blacks in the Revolutionary War	x			x				
Sweet Clara and the Freedom Quit	x			x			x	
If You Traveled on the Underground Railroad	x			x	x			
Ebony Sea				x	x		x	
The Story of Ruby Bridges				x				
A Picture Book of Rosa Parks		x		x			x	
If You Lived at the Time of Martin Luther King		x		x				
Pink and Say	x	x						
Black, Blue, and Gray: African Americans in the Civil War	x			x	x			

	1	2	3	4	5	6	7	8
Harriet Beecher Stowe: Author of Uncle Tom's Cabin (Famous Figures of the Civil War Era)	x			x				
Bound for America: The Forced Migration of Africans to the New World				x	x		x	
Coming to America: The Story of Immigration					x	x	x	
Journey to Ellis Island					x			
So Far from the Sea	x		x	x			x	
Faithful Elephants: A True Story of Animals, People, and War				x			x	
A Picture Book of Anne Frank	x				x			
The Wall			x	x				
The Vietnam Women's Memorial (Cornerstones of Freedom)				x			x	

	1	2	3	4	5	6	7	8
The Vietnam War (20th Century Perspectives)				x			x	
All by Herself: 14 Girls Who Made a Difference	x			x		x		
A Picture Book of Sojourner Truth				x		x		
Maya Angelou: Greeting the Morning	x	x	x	x			x	
Duke Ellington						x	x	
More Than Anything Else	x	x	x				x	
A Picture Book of George Washington Carver			x			x	x	x
Tallchief: America's Prima Ballerina	x			x		x		
A Picture Book of Sacagawea	x				x	x		
The Legend of the Indian Paintbrush	x					x		

Title Index

Subject Index

About the Authors

Deborah Ellermeyer is an assistant professor at Clarion University of Pennsylvania where she currently teaches courses in literacy and language arts methodology. She is a frequent presenter at international, national, state, and regional educational conferences. Ellermeyer is co-author of the teacher resource books, *Perfect Poems for Teaching Phonics* (Scholastic, 1999) and *Teaching Math with Favorite Picture Books* (Scholastic, 1998). Upcoming books include *Ancient Civilizations Readers Theater* (Creative Teaching Press, 2004) and *Sensational Sight Word Poems*: *20 Playful Poems with Activities That Teach Sight Words, Synonyms, Antonyms and More* (Scholastic, 2004).

Kay A. Chick has been an Assistant Professor of Curriculum and Instruction at Penn State Altoona since 1998. She holds a doctorate in elementary education from Indiana University of Pennsylvania and was a school psychologist for ten years. At Penn State, Dr. Chick teaches elementary and secondary education majors in the areas of educational psychology, educational theory and policy, and gender studies. She has had recent publications in the *Journal of Children's Literature,* the *Early Childhood Education Journal, Social Studies and the Young Learner,* and *Pennsylvania Reads: Journal of the Keystone State Reading Association.* This is her first book.